Mingled Waters

Mingled Waters

Sufism
& the Mystical Unity
of Religions

Pir Zia Inayat-Khan

Sulūk Press
New Lebanon New York

Published by Sulūk Press
an imprint of Omega Publications Inc.
New Lebanon NY
www.omegapub.com

Selection from *Memories of a Sufi Sage: Hazrat Inayat Khan* by
Sirkar van Stolk and Daphne Dunlop, 1967, reprinted by kind
permission of East-West Publication Fonds B.V.

Selections from *The Koran Interpreted* by A. J. Arberry, transla-
tor. Copyright © 1955 by George Allen & Unwin Ltd. Reprinted
with the permission of Scribner, a division of Simon & Schuster,
Inc. All rights reserved.

Cover background image from shutterstock.com
Cover design by Sandra Lillydahl
This edition is printed on acid-free paper that meets ANSI stan-
dard X39–48.

Inayat-Khan, Zia (1971–)
Mingled Waters
Sufism and the Mystical Unity of Religions
Includes preface, introduction, notes, bibliography, index
1.Sufism
I. Inayat-Khan, Zia II.Title

Library of Congress Control Number: 2017900168

Printed and bound in the United States of America

ISBN 978–1941810200 paper
ISBN 978–1941810217 hardcase

Toward the One,
the Perfection of
Love
Harmony
and Beauty

Contents

Contents

Preface

IN THE Name of God, the Most Merciful and Compassionate.

It is an occasion of great happiness that the blessed pen of the leader of the Chishtis in the West, my dear Pir Zia Inayat-Khan, is making a precious mark on the field of literature and culture. May it be a candelabrum of guidance and direction for seekers on the path of God, leading toward the goal of the saints and masters, which is to say, the knowledge of the presence of God. The way of the Sufis—whose draughts, as you will see, first aroused the thirst of Adam in the Garden of Paradise—is, on the battleground that is the world, the body of the soul. The shining rays of *Am I not your Lord?* (7:172) in the ear of the soul, abuzz with love and intimacy, are cast forth without consideration of this religion or that sect, this way or that school. Mystical unity is hidden from humans by the eyes of desire in the act of seeking.

> In the matter of rosewater and rose, this was
> the primal writ
> That would be the bazaar's darling, and this in
> seclusion would sit.
>
> (Hafiz)

Gnostics see the whole of the world as the manifesting place of the Friend. This vision is such that the prime matter of the spiritual unity of religions is deciphered in harmony and beauty. As Jami says:

> Waves of many colors are churned up in the sea,
> As color arises from the colorless deep.

The crashing waves of the ocean of the Water of Life and of the Holy Spirit consist of mystic souls, for wakefulness with regard to the multihued desires of that ocean is freedom, in Islamic mysticism as in all mysticism. In all of its seasons, the life of the human being is made smooth. Gnostics impress on human life this question: How is it that a human being, formed of flesh and skin ravaged by the four elements, stands like a drunkard on this Mount Sinai, calling out like Moses, *Show Yourself to me!* (7:143), and a melody ascends to the ineffable peak of Union and the Ka'ba of the Ipseity of God Most Holy? The Master of Balkh says:

> I was with Joseph in the well and beside Noah
> in the boat;
> I was in the fire with Abraham, I am the lover
> of old.

To conclude, it is, again, a matter of utmost happiness that in this age of computers, an era in which humankind is striving hard to conquer the planet Mars, this book guides the way for the searchers and seekers in the valley of gnosis. It is luminous, a radiant star on the path of the quest.

And success is only from God.

Sayyid Ahmad Shah Chishti Mawdudi
Spiritual Head, Central Chishti Lodge
Chisht Sharif and Herat, Afghanistan

Introduction

The true religion to a Sufi is the sea of truth,
and all different faiths are as its waves.
                                    —Hazrat Inayat Khan

SOMEONE ONCE offered the gift of a knife to Baba Farid. "Bring me a needle," he answered, "for the knife is a tool for cutting, while the needle is a tool for joining." The custom of the Sufis has always been to unite rather than to divide.

Mawlana Jalal ad-Din, the Shaykh of Rum, tells in his *Spiritual Couplets* of how a Persian, an Arab, a Turk, and a Greek received the gift of a *dirham* to share among them. The question immediately arose: what to buy with the coin? The Persian proposed *angur*, the Arab pressed for *'anab*, the Turk called for *uzum*, and the Greek insisted on *istafil*. Before long the group fell to blows. If only a speaker of many languages had been among them! He would have conciliated them and explained that they were of one mind in their desire for grapes.

As the story of the dirham shows, external divergences often conceal internal convergences. This is true of the revealed religions of the world. Exoteric distinctions tend to obscure the esoteric reality that the source and goal of all religions is the same. The Shaykh of Rum writes:

In the blessed salutations of the good and the true
The praises of the prophets are united through
    and through.
So many adorations are combined altogether,
Jugful after jugful in one ewer poured together.
Since the glorified one is not several but is one,
There is only one religion—beyond it there are none.

Water is water, whether drawn from a spring, pond, or river. Whatever jug it is poured into, water retains its identity. If a person is thirsty, the shape of the jug is of no consequence. All revelations descend from the One and reveal the presence of the One. Understanding this, the Sufi makes no distinction between God's messages, which are in reality one Message.

*We make no division between any of them, and to Him we surrender** (3:84)

"The Sufi's religion is God" is a saying of the shaykhs. The Shaykh of Rum explains, "The religion of love is distinct from all creeds; / God is the religion in which lovers believe."

Love's the sole religion of the people of the grape;
For us tepid sermons are a terrible headache.
(Qutb i-Din)

Muhyi ad-Din Ibn 'Arabi, the Greatest Shaykh, warns of the danger of narrowness in faith. He writes in his *Bezels of Wisdom*: "Beware of limiting yourself to a particular belief and denying all else, for much good would elude you; indeed the knowledge of reality would elude you. Be in yourself a substance for all

* This and all other quotations from the Qur'an are in italics and are from A. J. Arberry's translation.

forms of belief, for God is too vast and tremendous to be confined by one belief rather than another."

The shaykh's own faculty of spiritual perception expanded to such immense dimensions that he was moved to write:

> Amazing! A garden in the midst of the flames,
> My heart takes on the form of what it entertains:
> A meadow for gazelles, a Christian hermitage
> A pagan pagoda and the Hajj pilgrimage.
> It's the writ of the Torah and the Holy Qur'an;
> Love's faith is the path I'm bent to travel on.
> Down whichsoever path love's dromedaries speed,
> There's my religion; I profess that blessed creed.

Sufis recognize the diversity of revealed faiths as providential. Mansur Hallaj, the Martyr of Baghdad, once scolded an acquaintance for deriding someone's adherence to Judaism. When the man expressed his regret, Hallaj's demeanor softened and he explained, "My son, the religions, all of them, originate from God the Mighty and Majestic. He occupied every group with a religion, not of their own choice, but rather one chosen for them . . . I would have you know that while Judaism, Christianity, Islam, and all such religions may be different names and contrasting denominations, their goal admits of no difference or contrast."

> *If God had willed, He would have made you one nation*   (5:48)

> Waves of many colors are churned up in the sea
> As color arises from the colorless deep.
>   (Jami)

Abu Saʿid ibn Abiʾl-Khayr, the Shaykh of Mayhana, once visited a church in the company of his disciples. The congregation welcomed them with jubilation. When the shaykh departed, one of his disciples said to him, "If the shaykh had given a sign, they would have all untied their Christian sashes." Abu Saʿid answered, "As I did not tie their sashes, it was not for me to untie them."

ʿAyn al-Quzat, the Martyr of Hamadan, said, "If you too could see what the Christians see in Jesus, you would become a Christian: and if you too could see what the Jews see in Moses, you would become a Jew." All of the "seventy-two paths," he said, are way stations on the road to God.

> *Those who struggle in Our cause, surely We shall*
> *guide them in Our ways* (29:69)

> Every road I took led at last to Your address;
> You are the object, and existence is the quest.
> *(Dabistan-i mazahib)*

As the rivers of spiritual guidance flow briskly toward the ocean of divine Unity, their clear and sweet waters quench the thirst of all who long for truth and beauty. Sometimes the rivers meet, and where they do, there is *light upon light*. The pages that follow contemplate six holy waves and peer into a little handful of the sparkling drops they whirl along in their train.

WAVE ONE

Dreaming of India

The spirit of an elephant is wanted
To fly in sleep to Hindustan undaunted.

—*Rumi*

You who fault the Hindu on account of his icon,
Learn from him also how worship's to be done.

—*Amir Khusraw*

Be we Muslim, Mazdean, or perchance Hindu,
Whatever creed we follow, our faith is in You.

—*Baba Tahir*

LEGEND RELATES that when Adam was cast out of Eden he landed in India (specifically, on a mountain in Sarandib). There he repented, received good tidings from God, and became humanity's first teacher. Hence India is "the first place wisdom gushed forth."

Hazrat Inayat Khan wrote, "Sufism was intellectually born in Arabia, devotionally reared in Persia, and spiritually completed in India." Some speculate that the teacher of the early master Abu Yazid Bistami (d. 848 or 875) was a proponent of Vedanta. Husayn ibn Mansur Hallaj (d. 922) traveled to India in the ninth century. Afterward he visited Mecca wearing a patched shawl over his shoulders and an Indian loincloth around his waist. 'Ali Hujviri (d. bet. 1073 and 1077), author of the celebrated *Kashf al-mahjub* (*The Revelation of the Veiled*), settled in Lahore two centuries later. But it was not until the thirteenth century, with the arrival of Khvaja Mu'in ad-Din Chishti

(d. 1236) and his disciple Khvaja Qutb ad-Din Bakhtiyar Kaki (d. 1235), that Sufism firmly took root in Indian soil.

From the outset, Indian Sufism developed in dialogue with Hindu traditions. Treatises on yoga are attributed to Khvaja Mu'in ad-Din. Khvaja Qutb ad-Din's successor, Baba Farid (d. 1265), was known to converse with Nath Panthi yogis at his rural lodge in Ajhudan. Later writers credit Baba Farid with the introduction of a Hindavi invocation (*zikr*). His vernacular verses were preserved in the Sikh scripture, Guru Granth Sahib.

Baba Farid's successor, Khvaja Nizam ad-Din Awliya' (d. 1325), is remembered for the breadth of his sympathies. When he saw a group of Hindus worshiping on the banks of the Jumna, he observed, "For every people there is a religious path and a direction for prayer" (alluding to Qur'an 2:148). Khvaja Nizam ad-Din's disciple Amir Khusraw (d. 1325) studied Sanskrit and wrote verses in Hindavi. As a musician he synthesized Persian and Indian musical styles. The sitar is popularly regarded as Amir Khusraw's invention.

In the Mughal period it was not uncommon for authors associated with the Chishti and Shattari Orders to integrate Hindu motifs in their works. Shaykh 'Abd al-Quddus Gangohi (d. 1537) drew on the teachings of the legendary yogi Gorakhnath in his *Rushdnama* (*The Book of Guidance*). Shaykh Muhammad Ghaws Shattari (d. 1563) translated and expanded a syncretic Arabic treatise on yoga known as *Hawd ma' al-hayat* (*The Pool of the Water of Life*). Shaykh 'Abd ar-Rahman Chishti (d. 1683) composed a Sufi commentary on the Bhagavad Gita. Shah Nizam ad-Din Awrangabadi

4

(d. 1730) listed the "invocations (*azkar*) of the yogis" in his meditation manual *Nizam al-qulub* (*The Rule of Hearts*).

The emperor Akbar (r. 1556–1605) introduced a policy of religious pluralism under the slogan of "Universal Peace" (*sulh-i kull*). At the emperor's behest the Mahabharata, Ramayana, and other Sanskrit works were translated into Persian. Akbar's successor Jahangir (r. 1605–27) had the *Yoga Vasishtha* translated in abridged form. In his memoirs, Jahangir refers to Vedanta as the equivalent of Sufism.

Mughal interest in Hindu and Sufi mysticism reached its zenith in the singular life and work of Dara Shikuh (d. 1659), the eldest son and heir apparent of Jahangir's successor, Shah Jahan (r. 1627–58). A devoted disciple of the Qadiri masters Miyan Mir (d. 1635) and Mulla Shah Badakhshi (d. 1661), Dara Shikuh initially confined his spiritual studies within the horizons of Islamic Sufism. In time, however, he grew equally fascinated with the religious heritage of India. During this phase he commissioned a new translation of the *Yoga Vasishtha*. He went on to produce his own translations of the Bhagavad Gita and fifty-two Upanishads, which he accomplished with the assistance of a team of Hindu scholars. He also authored a unique comparative study of Sufism and Indian philosophy entitled *Majmaʿ al-bahrayn* (*The Merging of the Two Oceans*).

Whereas a combination of curiosity and political expediency guided Akbar's overtures toward Hinduism, a deeper passion drove Dara Shikuh. A vision of the sage Vasishtha and his disciple Rama prompted him to have the *Yoga Vasishtha* retranslated. He translated the

Upanishads because he believed these texts to be, "the first heavenly book ... not only in accord with the Glorious Qur'an, but a commentary on it." In the Upanishads Dara was convinced he had found the "hidden book" (*kitab al-maknun*) mentioned verse 56:78 of the Qur'an: a revelation containing the Qur'an itself, unreachable except by the pure.

The prince's translation of the Upanishads proved his final work. In 1658 his ambitious and puritanical brother Awrangzib (r. 1658–1707) rebelled against their ailing father and vanquished the imperial troops under Dara's command, sending the crown prince to flight. Awrangzib's forces at last captured him in Sindh. He was brought to Delhi, paraded through the streets in chains, and promptly put to death on charges of apostasy for the offense of describing Islam and Hinduism as siblings. Dara Shikuh's death marked the end of Akbar's legacy of Universal Peace and, arguably, the beginning of the Mughal Empire's long decline.

The judges who condemned Dara Shikuh championed an interpretation of piety that Dara deplored in his writings. In the introduction to *Majma' al-bahrayn* he confessed complete apathy toward the externalists of both the Islamic and Hindu faiths. He wrote in his *Divan*, "Paradise is a place in which there are no mullas." Defending Sufism against mulladom, he wrote:

> You say of the Sufis, "They have no religion,"
> But in fact they've attained religion's intention.
> A Sufi, you must realize, is not bound by creed;
> You're laboring under a misapprehension.

Yet for all the fateful friction between Dara Shikuh and the doctors of law, it cannot be denied that the prince's interpretations of Hinduism were consistently aligned with the monotheistic vision of the Qur'an. Dara maintained his Qur'anic reading of the Upanishads by construing the Sanskrit word *devas* (often translated in English as "gods") as *farishtagan* (angels) and *muvakkalan* (governing spirits). In *Majma' al-bahrayn* he identified Brahma, Vishnu, and Shiva with the archangels Gabriel (Jibra'il), Michael (Mika'il), and Seraphiel (Israfil). Such an interpretation finds its justification in the resounding emphasis in the Upanishads on the unity and primacy of Brahman. The Brahmanist monotheism of the Upanishads, in turn, has its foundation in the Vedic insight that, "The wise speak of what is One in many ways."

Among proponents of Sufism, Dara Shikuh was not alone in his monotheistic interpretation of Hindu theology. In the eighteenth century the Naqshbandi Shaykh Mirza Mazhar Jan-i Janan (d. 1781) warned against hasty judgments about Hindu beliefs and even took pains to justify the Hindu practice of idol veneration. He wrote:

> The reality of their veneration of idols is that they make and concentrate on idols representing some of the angels who exert influence in this world of existence and corruption by God's authority, or some of the spirits of saints which continue to have an influence in the universe after leaving the body, or some of those who, in their view, are immortal like Hazrat Khizr. By means of this concentration, after a time they establish a connection with the owner of the form and, by the power of

that connection, they fulfill their needs with respect to this world and the hereafter. This practice bears resemblance to *zikr-i rabita* (remembrance of the connection), whereby Muslim Sufis visualize the form of their teacher and obtain spiritual bounty from it. The only difference is that Muslim Sufis do not carve an image of their teacher. But this practice is not analogous to the creed of the Arab unbelievers.

In these lines, Mirza Mazhar Jan-i Janan draws a clear parallel between Hindu and Sufi contemplative practices. Certain Chishti shaykhs of the twentieth century went still further, not merely comparing Islamic and Hindu methods, but treating them as fundamentally the same. Shah Muhammad Taqi Niyazi of Bareilly (d. 1968), whose teachings contained allusions to the Upanishads and to various yogic disciples, glossed yoga as *suluk*, or "travel," a familiar synonym for Sufism. He wrote, "There is no difference between any of the prophets and guides who have passed through this world. One manifested love, another described the state of the spirit, and yet another described the One Essence without attributes." Khvaja Hasan Nizami (d. 1955) of Delhi, who wrote a biography of Krishna and an introduction to Hinduism, defined yoga as "the science of Sufism and dervishhood."

Nor was it solely in India that Indian mysticism spoke resonantly to the minds and hearts of Sufis. Sanusis in far-off North Africa adopted the yogic lore of the Shattaris. Shaykh Abdoulaye Dièye (d. 2002) of the Muridiya Order of Senegal was known to practice the chin mudra. He once declared, with a gleam in his eyes, "Whoever denies the truth of the Upanishads is a *kafir* (unbeliever)!"

> Many Turks and Hindus know how to speak
>   together,
> While many pairs of Turks are strangers altogether.
>   (Rumi)

DROP ONE

*Desire came
upon that one
in the beginning;
that was the first
seed of mind*

The Water of Life

WHAT EXISTED before the creation of the heavens and the earth? The Rig Veda gives an answer in the hymn known as the Nasadiya Sukta. As we must expect, it is an answer shrouded in mystery. The hymn begins:

> There was neither non-existence nor existence then; there was neither the realm of space nor the sky which is beyond . . . Was there water, bottomlessly deep?

God is said to be found in the conjunction of opposites. But in the beginning there were no opposites or differences of any kind. Being and nonbeing were unknown quantities. There was no here or there, no up or down, no inside or outside. What was there?

There was water. Muhammad, the Messenger of God, said, "God was, and there was nothing other than He. His Throne was on the water."

The heavens and the earth were a mass all sewn
up, and then We unstitched them and of water
fashioned every living thing   (21:30)

> Rain and clay and herbs and beasts
>   and the Perfect Human Being
> Were once a drop of water,
>   whence came every pictured thing
>   (Shabistari)

The hymn continues:

> There was neither death nor immortality then.
> There was no distinguishable sign of night nor of
> day. That one breathed, windless, by its own im-
> pulse.

The beginning had no end. Hence death and its overcoming were irrelevancies. No sun or moon rose or set there. And so Abraham, the Friend of God, said, *I love not those that set.*

"To the sage who has overcome limitations," observes Vasishtha, "there is neither day nor night."

> From beginning to end a single glory is seen,
> If you disregard the months and years in-between.
> (Dard)

"That one breathed." There was life and so there was breath. Breath that would one day enter Adam, the Pure in God. But "that one's" breath had no need of air. There was air neither above nor beneath the dark abyss. The hymn continues:

> Darkness was hidden by darkness in the
>   beginning.

Formless and bottomlessly deep, the Water of Life flowed silently in the Land of Darkness, where it still flows.

> Know that death is
>   the gathering of the nation,
> For darkness is
>   the *Aqua Vitae's* location.
> (Rumi)

Shah Kalim Allah, the Shaykh of Jahanabad, advises the seeker to visualize God as an ocean of light or else as pure and utter darkness. If as darkness, the Shaykh instructs, imagine yourself as a shadow losing itself in that boundless tenebrity. Blinding light and profound darkness have this in common: neither admits of multiplicity and both extinguish sight. The hymn continues:

> Desire came upon that one in the beginning; that was the first seed of mind.

God says, *I was a Hidden Treasure and I loved to be known, so I created the world that I might be known.* The One was alone, hidden away, and so, lonely. Desire arose: *ahbabtu an 'urafa*, "I loved to be known." *Hubb* means "love" and *habb* means "seed." Love was the first seed.

> *It is God who splits open the seed*   (6:95)

Out of the first seed came the tree called the Universe. From root to trunk to branch to leaf to blossom, from *lahut* to *jabarut* to *malakut* to *nasut*, this sprawling verdure in which we are perched is all the outgrowth of love. It is all mind, the many-tendriled, ever unfurling knowledge of what might be known. The hymn ends:

> Whence this creation has arisen—perhaps it formed itself, or perhaps it did not—the one who looks down on it, in the highest heaven, only He knows—or perhaps He does not know.

The ten outer and inner senses will at last exhaust themselves before penetrating the seventy thousand veils of light and darkness that conceal and reveal the One. "Contemplate the divine attributes but do not

15

contemplate the divine essence," said the Messenger. In all that concerns the ancient Source, "the inability to attain perception is itself perception."

> No one can know God by what is his own;
> God's essence is known to God's essence alone.
>
> (Sana'i)

Someone asked Abu'l-'Abbas Dinawari, "By what means do you know God?" He answered, "By means of the fact that I do not know Him." Hasan Basri inquired similarly of Rabi'a 'Adawiya, the Shaykha of Basra. She answered, "You know 'how'; I know 'without how.'"

As honest ignorance is a kind of knowing, a question is nearly as close to the answer as it is in a seeker's power to reach. But closer still is that ethereal quiet in whose hush every imaginable question and every conceivable answer is swept into the Void. "Whoso knows God his tongue is blunted," said the Messenger.

> Bring me, Saqi, the Water of Life,
> Bring a goblet of Life Forever;
> Bring that wine, I say, for without it
> Life animates none whomsoever.
>
> ('Iraqi)

DROP TWO

The eldest-born
being
is
Hiranyagarbha

The Great Soul

YOGA, THE YOKING of the finite to the Infinite, is an exceedingly ancient science. Its founder Hiranyagarbha, Golden Embryo, is designated in the Mahabharata as "the eldest-born being."

Dara Shikuh says, "From love the Great Soul appeared, which is to say the *jiv-atman*, which is called the 'Muhammadan Reality.' This alludes to the universal soul of the Chief of the Prophets, upon whom be peace and blessings. The monists of India call it 'Hiranyagarbha.'"

> The sun in the sky is the
>   mirror of his notions;
> The sea of existence is
>   the foam of his ocean.
>
> (Ishraq)

Contrary to the assumptions of materialism, consciousness is not a latecomer to the universe. Revelation, tradition, and unveiling confirm: the cosmos was endowed with a soul and a mind before it obtained its corporeal form.

> The wine became drunk with us, not we with it.
> The body transpired from us, not we from it.
>
> (Rumi)

At the dawn of creation, the Great Soul appeared. It is known as the Essence and the Intelligence. "The

19

first thing that God created was the Intelligence," said the Messenger. The Intelligence was the first instrument of Light, *a radiant lamp* to illuminate the path of existence. And so the Messenger said, "I was a prophet when Adam was between water and clay."

> The light in Adam's heart is you,
> The salve of every wound is you.
> O remedy for every pain,
> What everyone desires is you.
>
> (Ahmad)

Hiranyagarbha, says Shankaracharya, is "the inner soul of all." Within the subtle body of the Golden Embryo are strung together the subtle forms of all travelers through space and time, like pearls on the string of a necklace. Hence Hiranyagarbha, the Great Soul, is called *jiva-ghana*, the sum of spirits.

> What are the holy spirits? Exemplars of my essence. And the bodies of men? My embodiment's attendants.
>
> ('Iraqi)

The lineaments of the Great Soul's body are revealed in the contours of the heavens and the earth. The constellations in the night sky trace with their flickerings the outline of its colossal limbs. Mountains indicate its bones; rivers, its veins; and trees, its windswept hair. Its laughter rings out in thunder and its tears pour down in rain. Its beating heart is the Throne around which all turns. "The hearts of the faithful are the Throne of God," said the Messenger.

> This age-old body, which mere dust appears,
> Subsumes the vast secret lore of the spheres.
>
> (Bidil)

The human form is a miniature universe in which the whole of nature is drawn together. The *Taittiriya Upanishad* says, "From this very self did space come into being; from space, air; from air, fire; from fire, the waters; from the waters, the earth; from the earth, plants; from plants, food; and from food, man." Mu'in ad-Din Chishti, the Succor of the Poor, adds: "and from the essence of humanity comes the Perfect Human, and the essence of the Perfect Human is the Being of God."

> *The human is My secret and My description*
> (Hadith Qudsi)

Where is a Perfect Human to be found? Wherever the Great Soul, the Mirror of Eternity, alights. In the faces of the hundred and twenty-four thousand prophets and prophetesses who have walked the seven continents, from the Pure in God, Father of Humankind, to the Messenger, Father of Souls, the countenance of the Great Soul shines out. The saints too, God's friends, are known to bear this glow.

Were it not for the Perfect Human, the Hidden would have remained hidden. The stars that fill the cosmos are so many steps for the descent and ascent of the Great Soul. *But for you,* said God to the Light of the Prophet, *I would not have created the heavens.*

> God bless and keep the Prophet's Light
> From which all other lights descend;
> For love of him, the earth is still
> Entranced by him, the heavens wend.
> (Jami)

DROP THREE

Know therefore
that nature
is maya,
but that God
is the ruler
of maya

Maya

MAYA IS MAGIC that makes something seem other than it is. A conjurer's trick that draws gasps from a crowd is a good illustration of maya. But maya is not only at work when the laws of nature are confounded, or seem to be so. As the Vedas explain, nature itself is maya. By maya the One takes on the semblance of a multitude. The *Shvetashvatara Upanishad* explains:

> With maya He made all things, and by maya the human soul is bound. Know therefore that nature is maya, but that God is the ruler of maya.

How does unity produce multiplicity? Gaudapadacharya, in his *Mandukya Karika*, finds an answer in the phenomenon of motion. A glowing ember on the tip of a stick, held up in the darkness, appears as a point of light. But when the stick is twirled, the spinning ember gives rise to flashing shapes. In the same way, says the swami, the original Consciousness, *chitta*, gives rise to the illusion of numerous subjects and objects when set in motion.

> A subtle ruse, such is the world,
> Not unlike a spinning spark.
> Go whirl a firebrand at night,
> You'll see a circle in the dark.
> (Shabistari)

Motion makes a point appear as a circle and the One as the Many. What causes motion? Ibn 'Arabi, the Greatest Shaykh says, "The movement that is the being of the universe is a movement of love." The root of all motion is the movement of desire, the Hidden Treasure's desire to be known. Hence Dara Shikuh observes that maya is *'ishq*: love.

> Who is Adam? Who is Eve?
>   Both are love, without a doubt;
> Let a hundred million come,
>   Love is each who marches out.
>
> (*Wujud al-'ashiqin*)

The Hidden Treasure's desire to be known entails a descent into duality, which is a necessary condition for desire's progress through the stations of separation, longing, ascent, and union.

"Though unborn, It appears to be born in diverse ways," says the *Yajur Veda*. In reality, the Unborn never takes birth and duality is never more than a semblance. "He is now as He was." The spectacle of birth, death, and all that is between is a game played by the One.

> This "I" and this "we"—You set them in motion
> To play, with Yourself, the game of devotion.
>
> (Rumi)

An artifice, yes, but the Creator's creation is no mere *pastime*. Maya is only the means; devotion, gnosis and union are the end. To idle in desire's maze, vainly grasping at fleeting phantoms, is to stray far.

When *God has set a seal on their hearts* remembrance does not come easily. But there is hope, as the Bhagavad Gita announces: "Composed of Nature's qualities, My magic is hard to escape; but those who seek refuge in Me cross over this magic."

Therefore flee unto God! (51:50)

What, precisely, is to be crossed over? *Veda Vyasa*, bard of the Mahabharata, describes the entangling tree of Nature in this way:

> It is sprung from the Unmanifest, *Avyakta*.
> Its trunk is the intellect, the *buddhi*.
> Its cavities are the channels of the senses.
> Its branches are the great elements: earth,
>   water, fire, air, and ether.
> Its leaves are the objects of the senses.
> Its flowers are good and evil.
>
> This world is like a tree, O noble ones,
> And we are as its fruit—though unripe ones.
>
> (Rumi)

Those who seek refuge in the Opener of the Seed see beyond the clinging limbs of maya's tree. Abu Yazid, the Shaykh of Bistam, succeeded in making this escape. He became a bird whose body was made of oneness and whose wings were made of everlastingness. So doing, he flew until he reached the field of Forever and saw in its center the World Tree, root, branch, fruit, and all. He said, "I looked and I knew this was all a deception!" And he was free.

DROP FOUR

*Because He
craved for food
Brahman fashioned
this universe*

Food

"RESPECT BREAD," enjoined the Messenger. "One should not belittle food, that is the rule," agree the Vedic sages. If *'isha* and *'asha*—the evening prayer and the evening meal—arrive at once, tradition advises: begin with supper.

> A morsel is a seed, and thoughts are the fruits of it;
> A morsel is a sea, and thoughts are the pearls of it.
>
> (Rumi)

Food is the basis of life. Everything eats and is eaten in turn. Seeing this clearly a person might be moved to exclaim, "I am food! I eat him who eats the food!"

The physical body is a food body, composed entirely of what is eaten. Within it is a second body, made of a finer food. This is the body of *prana*, the breath of life. Breath, says Qushayri, is "the refreshment of hearts by means of subtleties from the Unseen."

The breath of life pervades material food as its *rasa*, its subtle essence. The rasa of the breath of life is mind, the rasa of mind is consciousness, and the rasa of consciousness is bliss. For every degree of essence there is a corresponding body. The body of bliss, residing innermost, is the essence of essences.

> *And when We let man taste mercy from Us, he rejoices in it.* (42:48)

31

Art is delicious food for the mind. Rapture comes when love is aroused in the spectator who forgets himself and imbibes what he sees and hears as though in a dream. The soul of rasa is delight.

No less than the seasoned palate or the cultured mind, the wakeful heart is an organ of tasting. "As the body's drink is water, the heart's drink is tranquility and sweetness," says 'Ali Hujviri.

Their Lord shall give them to drink a pure draught
(76:20)

The thirst of some drinkers is never quenched. The Shaykh of Bistam, Abu Yazid, said of himself: "Here is a man who, in a single day, gulps down the ocean of the eternity before time and the ocean of the eternity after time and cries out, 'Is there more?'"

Let me see You a thousand times a day,
And yet for one more glimpse still I will pray.
('Iraqi)

Concerning the wisdom of Hindustan, 'Aziz Nasafi observes, "The alchemy that a human being accomplishes is that, whatever he eats, he obtains its spirit and takes its cream and essence. In other words, he separates light from darkness in such a way that light knows itself and sees itself as it is."

Bees are always in quest of flowers. God teaches them by revelation to *eat all manner of fruit.* In their bellies the pollen of a thousand blossoms becomes a single golden liquid *wherein is healing for men.* Here is a manifest sign.

Whoever, like the bee, receives revelation,
Why shouldn't honey fill up his habitation?
(Rumi)

32

Just as the blossoms of innumerable trees become indistinguishable when reduced to honey, likewise tigers, lions, wolves, boars, worms, moths, gnats, and mosquitoes all in the end merge into the same essence, called the self, atman. Yajnavalkya says: "This self is the honey of all beings and all beings are the honey of this self." This self, this honey, is the essence of earth, water, fire, wind, the sun, the four quarters, the moon, lightning, thunder, space, law, truth, and humanity.

In short, everything in creation is fundamentally honey; everything is food. And know this: the ultimate eater of food is God. The *Maitri Upanishad* declares, "Because He craved for food Brahman fashioned this universe."

The Greatest Shaykh agrees:

> If for Himself God desires food,
>   For Him the universe is food;
> And if for us God desires food
>   Then, as He wills, He is the food.

The Creator nourishes creation and is nourished by it. God imparts to the world a mode of being, and the denizens of the world provide God a mode of knowing. "You are His food with respect to knowledge, and He is your food with respect to being," observes the Greatest Shaykh.

> Where is His self-sufficiency
>   When I help Him and rejoice Him?
> For this purpose God has made me:
>   To know and thus manifest Him
>
>   (Ibn 'Arabi)

O Believers, if you help God, He will help you

                                   (47:7)

When you eat food therefore, taste the essence of the essence of it, and lift your thoughts up to the Sustainer. So counsels the *Vijnana Bhairava*: "When one experiences the expansion of the joy of savor arising from the pleasure of eating and drinking one should meditate on the perfect condition of this joy, then there will be supreme delight."

What must have been the delight of the Messenger, who said, "I pass the night with my Lord, and he gives me food and drink"!

> Bread is God's greatest name—I had that realization,
> For it's the meeting point and religion's foundation.
> ('Attar)

DROP FIVE

*Know the self
as the rider
in a chariot,
and the body,
as simply
the chariot*

The Chariot

THE KATHA UPANISHAD relates a dialogue between the young Brahmin Nachiketas and Death. To
make up for an inadvertent lapse in hospitality, Death
offers Nachiketas three wishes. Nachiketas's first wish
concerns this world. He asks to be returned to his
father's good graces. His second wish pertains to the
hereafter. He asks to be taught the method of sacrifice
that leads to heaven. For his third wish, Nachiketas
aims higher. He wishes to know if the soul is immortal.

Death answers that to obtain sound knowledge, a
teacher is necessary. Thus the old saying, "He who
has no shaykh, his shaykh is Satan."

> Dress yourself in the color of your shaykh,
> From color to colorlessness make haste.
>
> (Ziya')

Eager for instruction, Nachiketas asks: "Tell me
what you see as / Different from the right doctrine
and the wrong; / Different from what's done here and
what's left undone; / Different from what has been
and what's yet to be."

> If you seek the secret of love
>   pass beyond unbelief and faith;
> For in the space where love is found,
>   unbelief and faith have no place.
>
> ('Attar)

37

Death is impressed that Nachiketas desires the good rather than the gratifying. He consents to reveal the mystery of life. Put simply, it is this: knowledge of the Supreme brings immortality. "The wise one—he is not born, he does not die."

> Be not without love, that you may not die;
> Die in love, that you may always survive.
> (Abu'l-Futuh)

For one who has died before death, the death of the body is merely a formality. To live in God is to live an endless life. When someone told Bu'l-Fazl Hasan that he had seen him in a dream laid out on a bier, the shaykh riposted, "Hush! That was yourself you saw in the dream. *They* never die."

> *And say not of those slain in God's way, "they are dead"; rather they are living, but you are unaware*
> (2:154)

> Never is there death for those whose hearts love's made alive,
> In the Book of Life their immortality's inscribed.
> ('Andalib)

The self that lives in God, the atman, is to the body as a rider is to a chariot. The intellect, buddhi, is the charioteer, and the mind, *manas*, makes up the reins. The organs of sensation are the horses that pull the chariot, and the objects of the senses are the roads the horses follow.

> With love our steeds galloped out
>   of nonexistence;
> With union's wine our night glowed
>   to incandescence.
> (Abu'l-Futuh)

As unruly stallions have their way with an inexperienced driver, the senses run wild when intellect lacks discernment. Only with reins firmly in hand can a chariot be driven to its intended destination.

When the chariot ascends the *straight path*, it traverses itself. The rider becomes the destination. The rider of the body is the soul and the rider of the soul is God. *Unto God is the homecoming.*

Above the senses are their objects and above these objects is the mind. Above the mind is the intellect, called "the essence," the *sattwa*. Above the intellect is the immense self, the *atma mahan*. Shankaracharya calls it "Hiranyagarbha, the Great Soul, the sum of spirits."

Above the immense self is the Unmanifest, *Avyakta*. Shankaracharya calls it "maya." Above the Unmanifest is the Person, *Purusha*.

> Higher than the Person there's nothing at all. That
> is the goal, that's the highest state.
>
> (*Katha Upanishad* 3)

The journey to God has an end, but the journey in God is endless.

The path to the One is as sharp as a razor's edge. To reach the goal, the mind must be brought into harmony with the essential intellect. That accomplished, the intellect must be submerged in the Great Soul. Finally, the Great Soul must be absorbed in the Infinite Person, called "the tranquil self."

> The way is easy, I want you to know,
> become the Shaykh, next the Prophet will glow.
> That station, in turn, likewise you'll forego;
> What more can I say? Truth's secret will show.
>
> (*Ziya'*)

> *O Soul at peace, return unto thy Lord, well-pleased,*
> *well-pleasing!*   (89:27)

While the confused desires of fools hasten their downfall, the wise seek and find what is stable, the smokeless light shining through the five senses, the "living, honey-eating self," *nearer . . . than the jugular vein.* In this ancient self, the sun rises and sets, and all the hosts of heaven are suspended. To affirm multiplicity and deny this unity is to wander "from death to death." All the while, "the Lord of what was and what will be" reigns forever, "changeless among the changing."

The Pure One "lies awake within those who sleep"; *slumber seizes Him not, neither sleep.* That unsleeping Lord is the breath of all breaths and the self in all selves. "So indeed is That!" The sheer force of That's glory makes fires blaze, the sun flash, and seraphs speed on their way. *The thunder proclaims His praise, and the angels, in awe of him.*

The intellect is a mirror of the universe, and the universe is the reflection of the Lord. "As in a mirror, so it is seen in the soul." "The faithful is a mirror of the Faithful."

> Nonbeing is the mirror of Infinite Being,
> For in it the Truth's bright reflection is seen.
> Nonbeing's the mirror, this world's the reflection,
> And we're the eye concealing the Person.
>   (Shabistari)

While the senses lurch and reel as the wheel of fortune turns, and sense-bound minds rise and fall in passions and disappointments, the self holds fast. The knower of the One, therefore, does not grieve.

Surely God's friends—no fear shall be on them,
   neither shall they sorrow   (10:62)

The highest state is reached by stilling the five senses and the mind, lulling the intellect to suspend its customary turnings. This is the yoga that *Patanjali* taught, the "cessation of thought" such that "the spirit stands in its true identity as observer to the world."

Mortal glances cannot possibly encompass the Subtle and Aware, but *He attains the eyes.* And the while the mind's thoughts are prone to stumble on the path, the heart's unveilings rise to the highest reaches of reality. God says, *Neither My heaven nor My earth embraces me, but the heart of my servant with faith does embrace me.*

> No one can see Him with his sight;
> With the heart, with insight, with thought,
> Has He been contemplated—
> Those who know this become immortal.
>   (*Katha Upanishad* 6)

WAVE TWO

Even unto China

Seek knowledge even unto China.

—Hadith

*Budhasaf and the Oriental sages before him said
that the Gate of Gates for the life of all elemental
castles is the human castle.*
—Shahab ad-Din Yahya Suhravardi

"SHAKYAMUNI IS TO THEM what the Prophet,
peace be upon him, is to us." So spoke the celebrated
Persian Sufi 'Ala ad-Dawla Simnani (d. 1336) concerning the followers of the Buddha. Simnani's knowledge
of Buddhism derived from his early years spent at the
Il-Khanid Mongol court. The scion of a prominent
family, Simnani enjoyed the confidence of the Buddhist
Il-Khanid ruler Arghun (r. 1284–91) and might have
comfortably lived out his days at the court but for a
mystical experience that convinced him to renounce
the luxuries to which he was accustomed in favor of
the pursuit of ultimate truth. In leaving the halls of
worldly wealth and power he followed in the footsteps
of the Buddha himself. He also followed the example
of Ibrahim bin Adham (d. 777–78), the Sufi paragon
whose legend echoes the story of the Buddha.

According to 'Attar's *Tazkirat al-awliya'* (*Memori-
al of God's Friends*) and other Sufi hagiographies,
Ibrahim bin Adham was king of Balkh until an inner

45

turn led him to take up the life of a wandering mendicant. Prior to its annexation by the Abbasid Empire in the eighth century, Balkh was a Buddhist stronghold. Its foremost monastery was called Naw Bahar, a Persian rendering of the Sanskrit words *nava vihara*, "new monastery." The keepers of Naw Bahar were a family known as the Barmakids (after the Sanskrit *pramukha*, "leader"). One line of this family converted to Islam and rose to prominence at the Abbasid court in Baghdad. Through the influence of Khalid ibn Barmak and his son Yahya ibn Khalid, Indian intellectual traditions became a subject of keen interest in Baghdad, and a number of Sanskrit texts were translated into Arabic. When the Barmakids fell into disgrace at the turn of the ninth century, however, the Baghdad-Balkh axis came to an end, and the attention of the Abbasids shifted to the Hellenistic West.

The Mongol conquest of the Persian and Arab heartlands in the thirteenth century brought Islam and Buddhism face-to-face again. The state policy of the Mongols promoted religious pluralism, and the adoption of Buddhism by Arghun, the second Il-Khanid ruler of Iran, elevated Buddhism to a powerful position. Though scant traces remain of Iranian Buddhism, Bausani speculates that during this time, "Iran must have been full of Buddhist temples."

Shaykh 'Ala ad-Dawla Simnani's discourses include interesting reflections on Buddhism as it was known and practiced at the Il-Khanid court. Particularly notable is Simnani's association with a Buddhist *bakhshi*, or monk, named Paranda (which means "bird" in Persian). Although he was of a foreign faith, Simnani speaks admiringly of Paranda:

He was a remarkable person and had accomplished much. To introduce himself to me he related this story. "I was the son of the king of a certain city in India. A state came over me causing me to turn away from the world and I renounced the exercise of governance. They directed me to an island in that vicinity where there lived a monk whose age was two hundred and fifty. He was perpetually in seclusion and had attained a sublime function. I fled and went there. For forty years I was in continuous seclusion. Extraordinary mystical experiences transpired and I ascertained the things of the monk's faith.

"I became intimate with the birds. Whenever the monk went out of the hermitage I sprinkled grain on my chest for the birds to eat. They became familiar with me. Then, unexpectedly, I became ill with an illness that did not improve with any form of treatment. The illness worsened to the point that news reached my homeland. My sister came and, with the monk's permission, brought me to the city. As many treatments as the doctors tried, none succeeded and the illness worsened. They said, 'This illness will not be cured unless you drink meat broth.' As eating meat is not allowed in our spiritual discipline (*suluk*), I declined and chose death over venturing into something foreign to our path (*tariq*). Finally my sister surreptitiously poured meat broth in my food and did not tell me. When I regained my health and rejoined my master (*pir*), one day I sprinkled grain on my chest as was my habit. None of the birds came; rather they fled from me. I told my master this. He said, 'They have tricked you. Find out what it is.'

"I went from there and pressed my sister to thoroughly explain. When she told me, I resolved to

undertake a pilgrimage (*hajj*) to expiate my sin."
It is to Somnath that they make pilgrimages. He
related, "I went to Somnath and saw monks and
ascetics there. They questioned me and asked
about my discipline and beliefs. I described them.
They were surprised, for they did not know this
path well and had become confused and brought
other beliefs into the path. Convinced of what
they thought, they did not like my path, and said,
'Your way resembles the way of the Muslims. The
way of Shakamuni is not what you describe. This
is the way of the Muslims.'

"I was surprised. I had never heard the name
'Muslims.' I said to myself, if Muslims have this
way, they must be a good people. Leaving the
monks and ascetics, I returned from Somnath to
rejoin my master. In the course of the journey an
adverse wind arose and sent the ship to shores of
Qatif and Bahrain.

"Entering their villages, I saw a strange people.
I asked, 'What people are these?' They said, 'Muslims.' I became happy and said to myself, 'I will see
to what extent it is so that, as they say, this path of
mine is their path.' I asked where their sages were.
They directed me to the people of learning. I went
and questioned them and explained to them the
states of this discipline. No one provided information or even knew. They forcefully brought me
from there to the court of Arghun. On the way I
reached the city of Shiraz. I said to myself, 'This
is a great city; perhaps they have information.'
Yet none of the scholars and worshipers whom I
questioned and interrogated had any information
about this inner path.

"I said to myself, 'How strange! They say, "your

discipline is the path of the Muslims," yet Muslims
have no news of it.'"

There is much that is remarkable in this narrative.
Like the Buddha, Ibrahim bin Adham, and Simnani
himself, Paranda is a mendicant who has renounced
a privileged life. The birds' aversion to Paranda after
he has unwittingly ingested meat is reminiscent of a
well-know story about Rabiʻa Basri (d. 801): when
Hasan Basri asked Rabiʻa why animals were so fond
of her, but fled from him, she answered, "You ate their
fat. Why wouldn't they flee from you?"

Most remarkable of all in Paranda's narrative is the
suggestion that Buddhism and Islam contain at their
respective cores inner paths that are not far apart,
though these paths are little understood by the exoteric authorities of both religions. Simnani concludes
his narration of the monk's story by commenting that
while Buddhism and Islam differ on several points,
they agree on the doctrines of resurrection, heaven
and hell, and the divine unity.

The dissolution of the Il-Khanate in the mid-four-
teenth century marked the end of the Pax Mongolica
that had enabled Buddhism to flourish in Iran. The
running encounter between Sufism and Buddhism
consequently shifted eastward. In seventeenth-century
Tibet, a master of the Naqshbandi Order was in touch
with the fifth Dalai Lama. In the following century,
a Muslim scholar named Khache Phalu produced
a popular Tibetan treatise on ethics that combined
monotheism and reverence for the Buddha. During
the same period in China, authors such as Wang Tai-
Yü and Liu Chih (d. 1730) composed Sufi treatises

that drew upon the terminologies of Confucianism, Taoism, and Buddhism.

In 1923, during a tour of the United States, Hazrat Inayat Khan (d. 1927) was introduced to the Rinzai Zen monk Nyogen Senzaki (d. 1958) in San Francisco. Soon after, Senzaki Roshi penned an article for the *Japanese American* describing their interactions, entitled "Mohammedan Zen: Sufism in America." Senzaki's vignettes are a charming installment in the chronicle of Sufi-Buddhist contacts down the centuries.

> Zen is not confined to Buddhism. In Christianity there is an element of Zen. It also appears in Taoism and in Confucianism, however colored by those respective schools of thought. Mohammedanism is supposed to be monotheistic, but its offspring which calls itself "Sufism" encourages introspection among its students so as to realize Allah, or God, within one's inner self. If the thoughts of St. Bernard and of Meister Eckhart can be called "Zen," then the ideas of Jalal ad-Din Rumi of Persia, as well as those of Kabir, the Indian poet, may also be called "Mohammedan Zen."
>
> . . .
>
> Inayat Khan smiled at me and asked, "Mr. Senzaki, will you tell me what the significance of Zen is?" I remained silent for a little while, and then smiled at him. He smiled back at me. Our dialogue was over.
>
> . . .
>
> His eyes were full of water—not the tears of the world, but water from The Great Ocean—calm and transparent. I recited an old Zen poem—not

with my mouth—not in thought, but with a blink, like a flash. It reads:

No living soul comes near that water—
A vast sheet of water as blue as indigo.
The abyss has a depth of ten thousand feet.
When all is quiet and calm at midnight,
Only the moonlight penetrates through the
    waves,
Reaching the bottom easily and freely.

"Murshid," said I, "I see a Zen in you." "Mr. Senzaki, I see a Sufism in you," he replied. Both of us then smiled at each other.

. . .

I noticed that the Murshid uses the Nyaya system of logic in making affirmations, and this made me feel very much at home with him, as we Buddhists use the same system.

. . .

It was about two o'clock in the afternoon, and the Murshid asked me to meditate with him in a secluded room where his pupils received personal guidance. We sat down to meditate together, but before even one stick of incense was consumed, both of us must have entered into Samadhi, for Mrs. Martin suddenly called us, stating that it was already dark, time for us to go home for our respective dinners. We looked at each other with surprise, but nodded a knowing assent to each other. The incense had been completely consumed so long that no fragrance remained in the room. Both Sufism and Zen had become, after all, only yesterday's dream.

. . .

At the corner of the street where I was about to bid the Murshid goodbye, I remarked, "All sounds return to one, and where does that one go?" Inayat Khan stopped walking and, shaking hands with me, responded, "Goodnight, Mr. Senzaki."

DROP ONE

*Difficult is
the attainment
of the
human state*

*Difficult the
appearance of
Awakened Ones*

Awakening

SIDDHARTHA GAUTAMA was born to Queen Maya and King Shuddhodana in a garden grove in Lumbini. Legend relates that he emerged from his mother's right side: the seat of the *latifa ruhiya*, the subtle organ of spirit. Two streams of water, resembling solar and lunar rays, poured down on his fontanel from the heavens. The angels rejoiced, the sun shone brighter, soothing breezes blew, a well sprang up, and the ferocious beasts of the forest were pacified.

> In that meadow springs flow everywhere,
> And animals dwell without a care.
>
> (Rumi)

The sage Asita saw by inner sight that this child was destined to become an *awakened one*, a buddha. As Prince Siddartha grew, his father's kingdom flourished. So great did the prince's splendor wax, "Queen Maya could not bear the delight it caused her; so she departed to dwell in heaven."

To shelter the prince from the suffering of the world, King Shuddhodana assigned rooms for him on the upper floors of the palace. Young Siddhartha was married to the beautiful princess Yashodhara and surrounded with enchanting handmaidens. Every kind of sensual pleasure was supplied for his enjoyment.

> If you say you'll quit this wine for a time,
> You'll dip your lips in eternity's wine
>
> (Rumi)

Prince Siddhartha's gaiety was shattered when he ventured out from the palace at last. While riding through the city streets he witnessed first a man bent low with age, then a sufferer of grave illness, and finally a corpse on a bier. *Surely death, from which you flee, shall encounter you.* Quickly deducing that old age, illness, and death must eventually be his own fate, all enthusiasm for the world drained out of him.

> The wheel of fortune, alas, has no other end
> Than the function of separating friend from friend.
>
> (*Anvar-i suhayli*)

The Messenger said, "Death suffices as a warner." If the sight of death does not blanch the face of a careless reveler, nothing will. Mutarrif ibn 'Abd Allah remarked, "This death has indeed spoilt the pleasure of those preoccupied with pleasure, so seek out that pleasure in which there is no death." Shibli consoled a bereaved man saying, "Choose another friend, one who will not die."

> The demise of your friends is always a death to
>   you too;
> To pin your heart on a mortal is an odd thing to do.
>
> (Nakhshabi)

Utterly disillusioned, Prince Siddhartha left in the night, vowing not to return to his father's city until he had seen "the farther shore of birth and death." After passing through the ascetic grove outside the city gates he sought guidance at the hermitages of the sages Arada and Udraka. But he found their teachings incomplete and did not stay long. Taking another course, with five mendicants for companions he applied himself to mortifications in the forest. In this way he grew emaciated, but peace proved elusive.

> The ascetic is like a grim reaper
> Who keeps slashing himself, ever deeper.
>
> ('Attar)

On perceiving the futility of asceticism, Siddhartha abandoned it and restored his body to health. He was intent now to follow the Middle Way between the extremes of sensuality and self-mortification. *Surely my Lord is upon a straight path.* With firm resolve, he sat cross-legged under a banyan tree and vowed, "I'll not break this posture on earth until I have fulfilled my task."

Shibli observes, "Sufism is sitting in the presence of God Most High without sadness."

Mara, the tempter, was troubled to find Siddhartha so closely nearing his goal. Summoning his sons (Fluster, Thrill, and Pride), his daughters (Discontent, Delight, and Thirst), and an army of fiendish djinn, he sought to lure Siddhartha off course with honeyed promises. When coaxing failed, in a rage he unleashed a maelstrom of abuse. Through it all, Siddhartha remained impassive.

> The devil and the ego are one and the same;
> They differ only as pertains to form and name.
>
> (Rumi)

God asked the Shaykh of Bistam, "What do you want?" He answered, "I want not to want."

When the storm passed, all was quiet. Siddartha fell into deep absorption. In a single sweep, he recalled the whole of his past. The panorama before him drew from his breast a wave of compassion for all beings. He saw that for all its apparent substantiality, the world was hollow at its core, like a banana tree.

"There is nothing inside this robe but God," declared Abu Sa'id, the Shaykh of Mayhana.

In the second watch of the night, Siddhartha witnessed the births and deaths of innumerable creatures on all planes of being. He observed the torments of hell and the delights of paradise, and saw how the denizens of both realms reaped the harvest of their actions.

> *If you do good, it is your own souls you do good to,*
> *and if you do evil it is to them likewise.*   (17:7)

> Each fool that sows the seed of someone's sorrow
> Will reap a bitter harvest on the morrow.
> (Anvar-i suhayli)

In the third watch, Siddhartha contemplated the genesis of the phenomena of the world. At the root of all contingent and ephemeral accidents of being he discerned *avidya*, ignorance. From ignorance sprang up *samskaras*, formations caused by volition—shapes of desire.

> Being desire from heat to foot made us slaves
>   from the start;
> We would have been God but for the desire in our
>   hearts.
> (Mir)

Volitional formations give rise to individual consciousness, and individual consciousness precipitates name-and-form. Name-and-form, the self or *nafs*, is the foundation of the six sensory fields: touch, taste, smell, hearing, sight, and mind. The six senses lead to contact, contact produces feeling, and feeling spawns craving. Craving results in clinging, and this sets in motion the cycle of becoming. Becoming involves birth, and birth inevitably leads to aging and death, sorrow, lamentation, pain, dejection, and despair.

> When there was nothing, there was God;
> Should there be nothing, God would be.
> I've been drowned by my existence;
> Had I not been, what then would be?
>
> (Ghalib)

Throwing off the bonds of ignorance and its offshoots, with clear eyes Siddhartha witnessed the insubstantiality of all and everything, including himself.

> You saw the world, and all you saw was nothing;
> And all you said and heard, that too was nothing.
>
> (Khayyam)

In the fourth watch of the night, as the sun peered over the eastern horizon, Siddhartha attained realization of the Unconditioned, *as-Samad*, and was awakened. He was known thereafter as *Tathagata*, He Who Has Thus Gone.

His quest had been arduous, but what in this world is not difficult—if not at first, sooner or later? And with the tranquility of awakening comes the end of difficulty. The Buddha reflected:

Difficult is the attainment of the human state.
Difficult is the life of mortals.
Difficult is the hearing of the dharma true.
Difficult the appearance of Awakened Ones.

It's difficult for every kind of task to be easy;
Even for a man to become human is not easy.
                                        (Ghalib)

DROP TWO

There is the Unborn,
the Ungrown,
and Unconditioned

Steps to Freedom

IN THE DEER PARK in Sarnath, He Who Has Thus Gone turned the wheel of the dharma. The Buddhas of prior ages had taught a path of eight divisions. He Who Has Thus Gone now revived it. The divisions are right view, right intention, right speech, right action, right livelihood, right effort, right mindfulness, and right concentration.

Right view means seeing things as they are. This has two degrees, one mundane and the other superior. Mundane right view consists in understanding the law of karma, which is to say, recognizing that the actions of all sentient beings return to them.

Whosoever trespasses the bounds of God has done wrong to himself. (65:1)

He Who Has Thus Gone said, "By oneself is wrong done, by oneself one is defiled. By oneself wrong is not done, by oneself, surely, one is cleansed." *Shall the recompense of goodness be other than goodness?* The Messenger said: "Certainly they are your actions that come back to you."

> By his own misfortune is a man done in;
> From ourselves to ourselves, so our doings spin.
> (Nakhshabi)

Right view in its mundane degree motivates a person to perform wholesome actions in order to enjoy wholesome fruits. For seekers of paradise, this is sufficient. But seekers of the truth aim higher.

> While sinners repent of sinful errors,
> Gnostics repent of imperfect prayers.
>
> (Sa'di)

Abu Bakr Kattani said, "The Sufi is one who regards his devotions as an offence for which he must ask forgiveness."

Right view in its superior degree brings the understanding that the rewards of paradise are, in the last analysis, only loftier veils. What is wanted is the luminous unveiling of the Sublime. "There is no rest for the faithful but in the encounter with God," said the Messenger.

> Everyone pleads his need at Your door;
> You are my need; I've come to implore.
>
> ('Andalib)

The Shaykha of Basra, Rabi'a 'Adawiya, prayed, "O Lord, if I worship You for fear of hell, burn me in hell, and if I worship You in hope of heaven, bar me from heaven; but if I worship You for Your own sake, do not deny me Your everlasting beauty." She was seen walking with a bucket of water and a torch—to extinguish hell and burn down paradise.

Concerning God's loyal friend Ma'ruf Karkhi, it is expected that on the Day of Judgment the angels will have to usher him into heaven shackled in chains of light, while he protests, "I did not worship You for the sake of heaven!"

> Without the Beloved's intimacy
> The highest heaven means nothing to me.
>
> (Nakhshabi)

In the Beloved's absence, paradise is a prison. He Who Has Thus Gone said, "Who, having abandoned the human bond, has transcended the heavenly bond, who is released from all bonds, that one I call a Brahmin."

> It is Layla herself we are searching for;
> Paradise is an orchard and nothing more.
>
> (Chishti)

Only in the Unconditioned are all longings quelled. He Who Has Thus Gone explained:

> O monks, there is the Unborn, the Ungrown, and Unconditioned. Were there not the Unborn, the Ungrown, and Unconditioned, there would be no escape for the born, grown, and conditioned. Since there is the Unborn, the Ungrown, and Unconditioned, so there is an escape for the born, grown, and conditioned.

> *There was no shelter from God except in Him*
> (9:118)

The second division of the Noble Path, right intention, consists of the triple intention of renunciation, good will, and harmlessness. Renunciation entails freeing oneself from dependence on worldly pleasures. Such dependence fuels all kinds of selfish acts and inevitably leads to suffering.

> What makes a human being sink down to beastliness?
> Neediness, neediness, the answer is neediness.
>
> ('Andalib)

Fuzayl ibn 'Iyaz remarked, "God placed all evil in a certain house and made its key love of the world; and God placed all goodness in another house and made its key renunciation."

You will not attain the good until you expend of
what you love   (3:392)

'Aziz Nasafi observes, "For a person in this world who is seized with a desire, hidden under that desire are a hundred undesirables." They asked the Shaykh of Bistam by what means he had attained his high station. He answered, "By nothing." They asked, "How so?" He answered, "I understood with certainty that this world is nothing."

Good will means establishing love in the heart so completely that all traces of malice are obliterated. The One says, *My mercy embraces all things.* Those who are near and dear to the One therefore embody the traits of mercy: riverine generosity, sunny affection, and earthy humility.

To practice harmlessness is to take no pleasure in the pain of others and do nothing that will cause anyone hardship. The life of mortals has tribulations enough without our unnecessarily adding to them. He Who Has Thus Gone taught, "Not by enmity are enmities quelled, whatever the occasion here. By the absence of enmity are they quelled. This is an ancient truth. Others do not realize, 'We are here struggling.' Those who realize this—for them are quarrels therefore quelled."

As for he who put thorns in my path for sheer spite,
May roses bloom thornless in the garden of his life.
(Abu Sa'id)

Shantideva expresses the same prayer:

All those who slight me to my face
Or do me some other evil,

> Even if they blame or slander me,
> May they attain the fortune of enlightenment!

Nizam ad-Din Awliya' remarked, "The way of people is that with the sincere you are sincere and with the crooked you are crooked, but the way of dervishes is that, whether you are with the sincere or the crooked, you are sincere." Why, after all, should one emulate someone's crookedness?

The chevalier has no enemy. In the battle of life victory comes only to the self-conqueror. The Shaykh of Kharaqan, Abu'l-Hasan, declared, "I have made peace with God's creation and will never wage war with it; and I have waged war with my ego and will never make peace with it."

The ego is brought to heel when one carefully observes one's own thoughts and deeds rather than dwelling on others' shortcomings. "Easily seen is the fault of others, but one's own is hard to see," said He Who Has Thus Gone.

> Heedless of myself, I was once quick to judge others;
> But none seem flawed now that I've seen my own blunders.
>
> (Zafar)

Right speech means abstaining from deceit, slander, harsh words, and idle chatter. To say only what is true is a requisite of the path of truth. The seeker must refrain absolutely from maligning people, spreading rumors, and otherwise sowing dissention. Speech should be gentle, considerate, and gracious. Empty banter is wasted breath.

> *A good word is as a good tree*   (14:24)

Two intelligent people do not bicker as a rule,
Nor does someone who is wise choose to wrangle
    with a fool.

(Sa'di)

Right action means abstaining from the taking of life, the taking what is not given, and the illicit indulgence of lust. He Who Has Thus Gone said, "By harmlessness toward living beings is one called a Noble One." This is the teaching of the prophets. Abu'l-Hasan, the Shaykh of Kharaqan, said, "Whoever passes a whole day without harming anyone, it is as though he has spent that day with the Messenger."

Right livelihood means earning one's living in a manner that is just and fair. Ill-gotten gains are no gains at all. Only "righteous wealth righteously gained" brings peace. Honest work is in the natural order of things. *We appointed day for a livelihood.*

Right effort means rousing oneself to cast off unwholesome states of mind and to cultivate wholesome ones. That is to say, the seeker must refrain not only from destructive actions, but also from clumsy thoughts and emotions. This requires firm determination. *Those who struggle in Our cause, surely We shall guide them in Our ways.* "One who does not stand at the outset will not find a seat at the conclusion," remarked Abu 'Ali Daqqaq.

On the path of God, O soldier, reach higher;
Without ambition honor can't be acquired.

(Sana'i)

Right mindfulness consists in attentive contemplation of the body, of feelings, of the mind, and of phenomena. Awareness of the body begins with awareness of the breath. The People of the Way deem counting one's breaths with God to be the best of all acts of worship. Shibli said, "Sufism is the subdual of the faculties and the observance of the breaths."

> Every breath of your life is a jewel in sooth;
> Every atom within you a guide to the truth.
>
> ('Attar)

'Abd Allah Faraj said, "Over a single day and night I counted fourteen thousand blessings of a single kind." Someone asked, "How did you reach that figure?" He answered, "I counted my breaths in the course of a day and night. There were fourteen thousand breaths."

Next one should sustain awareness of one's posture, whether walking, sitting, standing, or lying down. In this connection, Fatima bint Abi'l-Mutanabbi said of the Greatest Shaykh, "When he stands, he stands with the whole of himself; and when he sits, he sits with the whole of himself."

One should be attentive to one's actions and perform them in a serenely impersonal state of mind. Recall that God said to the Messenger, *When thou threwest, it was not thyself that threw, but God threw.* The Martyr of Baghdad, Mansur Hallaj, observes, "As a servant does not possess the root of his act, so he does not possess the act itself."

Having attained detachment with respect to actions, the seeker should contemplate the body as mass of skin, hair, nails, flesh, bone, blood, bile, phlegm, and so forth. The expected result is a feeling of detachment from this not-so-pretty bag of bones. The next step is to observe how the various constituents of the body are all permutations of the four elements: earth, water, fire and air. Where in all of this is justification for an ego?

> The elements are four birds bound with one tie;
> Let death cut the cord and away they will fly.
>
> (Rumi)

To complete the contemplation of the body, the seeker should graphically imagine death. No detail should be omitted, from the stopping of the heart to the final stages of the body's decomposition. In this way the seeker anticipates the inevitable and recognizes that it is not far off. "Die before you die," instructed the Messenger. "When you remember the departed reckon yourself as one of them," remarked Abu'l-Darda.

> When you give up your life before Death beckons,
> You pass beyond both the earth and the heavens.
>
> (*Wujud al-ʿashiqin*)

The contemplation of the body leads on to the contemplation of feelings. As the senses come into contact with a variety of objects, the seeker should observe the feelings that arise, whether pleasant, painful, or neutral. As a further step, the seeker should attend to the states of mind underlying these feelings. This process of *sati*, or mindfulness, culminates in the clear awareness of all manner of phenomena, both favorable and unfavorable. Here the seeker beholds directly the five hindrances: sensual desire, ill will, dullness and drowsiness, restlessness and worry, and doubt—as well as the seven factors of enlightenment: mindfulness, investigation, energy, rapture, tranquility, concentration, and equanimity.

> *Surely God is witness of everything*   (33:52)

Murta'ish explained vigilance as, "watching one's inner being in order to be mindful of the hidden every moment and with every word spoken."

> Though *God's face* manifests in every nook,
> Within your self is the best place to look.
>
> (Bidil)

Right concentration, the eighth division of the Noble Path, calls for the unification of consciousness. Right concentration has eight stages, the first four involving form and the latter four transcending form. Through these stages the seeker ascends through the planes of abstraction, in keeping with the dictum of Junayd: "Unification is the isolation of the eternal from the originated."

In the four "absorptions with form," the seeker first attains rapture, happiness, and one-pointedness by means of a mental gesture, and then learns to dispense with the gesture. The Shaykh of Kharaqan observes, "An hour in which the servant is happy with God is more precious than years of prayer and fasting."

> Enjoy this moment with fullness of presence,
> For this moment is life's very quintessence.
>
> (Khayyam)

Eventually the feeling of rapture fades away and is succeeded by a subtler sense of equanimity and mindfulness. This condition in turn gives way to a state of purity devoid of pleasure or pain.

> The one the beauty of the Friend intoxicates
> Stands exempt from injury at the hand of fate.
>
> (Mas'ud)

This is the sphere of infinite space. Becoming in this way a "monarch on the throne of awareness," the seeker is now ready for the four formless absorptions. In the formless absorptions, the seeker initially beholds infinite consciousness and then, proceeding further, discovers the sphere of nothingness.

> The world exists because of you and me;
> If there are no waves, then there is no sea.
>
> (Bidil)

Beyond the sphere of nothingness, the seeker enters the sphere of "neither-perception-nor-non-perception." Finally, the seeker's ascent to unity culminates in the cessation of perception and feeling: nirvana.

> Becoming of self entirely free,
> I'll selflessly reach God's eternity
>
> ('Attar)

"The conditioned becomes the Unconditioned," declares Jami. But here, language becomes bewildered and words prove powerless.

> Your loveliness exceeds my sight,
> Your secret dwells beyond my lights.
> My self's a crowd, while I want You!
> To tell of You I lack the might.
>
> (Abu'l-Futuh)

DROP THREE

*No beings at all
have been led to
nirvana*

Paradox

ONE DAY, He Who Has Thus Gone was seated in Jeta Grove outside the city of Shravasti, attended by a group of monks. One of the monks, the Venerable Subhuti, approached him with reverence and asked how seekers pursuing the Noble Eightfold Path should progress and control their thoughts. He Who Has Thus Gone's answer has been passed down to posterity as the *Diamond Sutra*.

> Someone who has set out in the vehicle of a Bodhisattva should produce a thought in this manner: "As many beings as there are in the universe of beings . . . all these I must lead to Nirvana, into that realm of Nirvana which leaves nothing behind."

> In the path of the Friend I am so drunk with passion,
> My comrades are swooning by force of attraction.
>   (Bidil)

A voice once came to the Succor of the Poor, Mu'in ad-Din Chishti, from the Invisible, saying, "You who breathe with Me, I will grant whatever you request." The saint answered, "Gracious Lord, confer Your grace on my disciples, on my disciples' disciples, and on all who join this tree." The voice assented: "Those who come on your account, to them will be Our Hand held out."

Commencing with those who seek their guidance, the friends of God strive to lift up all beings. Since all creatures belong to the One, the servant of the One is concerned with the welfare of them all, without exception. Shibli declared, "A Sufi is not a Sufi until he takes upon himself the whole of creation as a family charge."

> And yet, although innumerable beings have thus been led to nirvana, no being at all has been led to nirvana.
>
> (*Diamond Sutra* 3)

Why? Because, in truth there are no *beings*—only *Being*.

> This talk of bodies and planes is all too peripheral,
> Let's be done with animal, vegetable, and mineral.
> There is but one Essence, though its attributes vary;
> And so people imagine the One as the several.
>
> (Jami)

> A Bodhisattva who gives a gift should not be supported by a thing, nor should he be supported anywhere.
>
> (*Diamond Sutra* 4)

Whatever is done egoistically, however seemingly fine a deed, runs counter to the goal of selflessness. Kindnesses proudly bestowed become blocks in the prison walls of the illusory self. Ruwaym said, "Sincerity is lifting of one's sight from the act."

> Wherever there is possession of marks, there is fraud; wherever there is no-possession of no-marks, there is no fraud.
>
> (*Diamond Sutra* 5)

> What of Adam, the world, and the marks thereof?
> We are purely the dew of the mist of love.
>
> (Qutb-i Din)

> And these Bodhisattvas . . . will not be such as
> have honored only one single Buddha, nor such
> as have planted their roots of merit under one
> single Buddha only.
>
> (Diamond Sutra 6)

The prophets and messengers of all lands form a
single lineage of wisdom. Each one revived the Message
of the ones who came before. *We make no distinction
between any of them, and to Him we surrender.*

> This dharma which the Tathagata has fully known
> or demonstrated—it cannot be grasped, it cannot
> be talked about, it is neither a dharma nor a
> non-dharma. And why? Because an Absolute exalts
> the Holy Persons.
>
> (*Diamond Sutra 7*)

Dharma and non-dharma, faith and infidelity—these
categories pertain to the topography of multiplicity,
the coordinates of which are separate selves. When the
knowledge of unity arrives, all such contraries are reconciled in the Absolute.

> It's your ego that brings in faith and infidelity;
> Such distinctions color your vision most definitely.
> Eternity is void of creeds and infidelity;
> Such things don't exist in the primordial purity.
>
> (Sana'i)

Shibli remarked, "Sufism is polytheism, because it
is guarding the heart against the sight of the other,
and there is no other."

> If . . . it would occur to an *Arhat*, "by me has Arhat-
> ship been attained," then that would be in him a
> seizing on a self, seizing on a being, seizing on a
> soul, seizing on a person.
>
> (*Diamond Sutra 9*)

To be an arhat—an *'arif*, a gnostic—is to be conscious of the Unconditioned, and to be conscious of the Unconditioned requires the abandonment of all preening self-regard. Sufyan Sawri said, "If someone says to you, 'What an excellent man you are,' and you are more pleased than if he had he said, 'What a bad man you are,' know that you are still a bad man."

> The Bodhisattva, the great being, should produce an unsupported thought . . . a thought unsupported by sights, sounds, smells, tastes, touchables, or mind-objects.
>
> (*Diamond Sutra* 10)

A thought that is independent of the ten outer and inner senses is a thought that rests purely on the Unconditioned, a perception surpassing time, space, and every conceivable distinction. Abu Hashim Madani said, "If the eyes had eyes, they could not see the rapidity of my steps."

"They do not rest on anything, like a bird in the sky—this is the abode of those who are perfect in knowledge," observes Sudhana. *Naught holds them but God.*

> I am the Old Bird that lives in No Place;
> Without feather or wing, I soar through space.
>
> (Sufi)
>
> When the king of Kalinga cut my flesh from every limb, at that time I had no perception of a self.
>
> (*Diamond Sutra* 14)

At the Battle of Uhud, 'Ali, the Lion of God, was struck by an arrow. The arrowhead proved difficult to remove. They waited until he was absorbed in prayer and then extracted it unbeknownst to him. When his prayer was finished, they explained what they had done. He said, "When I am in intimate conversation, whether spears rain down on me or the world turns upside down, I am oblivious to the world and its lights on account of the pleasure of my converse with God."

> Said the Lion to the Most High,
> I felt no pain during that time.
>
> (Sana'i)

> 'Tathagata' is called one who has not gone anywhere, nor come from anywhere.
>
> (*Diamond Sutra* 29)

They asked Shibli, "What is Sufism?" He answered, "It is that you should be such as you were on that day when you were not."

> Nothing could be better in this house of woe
> Than neither to come, to tarry, nor to go.
>
> (Khayyam)

> As stars, a fault of vision, as a lamp,
> A mock show, dewdrops, or a bubble,
> A dream, a lightning flash, or cloud,
> So should one view what is conditioned.
>
> (*Diamond Sutra* 32)

Phenomena transpire, alter, unravel, and vanish with such mercurial capriciousness that nothing that stirs the senses can be credited as a solid fact. Stars fade, lamps fizzle out, moisture evaporates, bubbles burst, and clouds disperse while, all the while, the Absolute endures unchanged.

> *All that dwells upon the earth is perishing, yet still abides the face of thy Lord, majestic, splendid*
>
> (55:26–27)

DROP FOUR

Form does not differ from emptiness

Form and Emptiness

HE WHO HAS THUS GONE was seated in meditation on Vulture Peak in Rajagriha, absorbed in the perception of the profound. Around him were assembled numerous monks and bodhisattvas. The bodhisattva Avalokiteshvara was "moving in the deep course of wisdom." Surveying the world from on high, he beheld but five heaps: matter, sensations, perceptions, mental formations, and consciousness. And he saw that in their own-being they were empty.

> "Why is the path so empty?" wondered a bird;
> Said the hoopoe, "for the glory of the Lord."
>
> ('Attar)

He Who Has Thus Gone invisibly directed the Venerable Shariputra to put a question to Avalokiteshvara. Shariputra accordingly asked Avalokiteshvara how the perfection of wisdom should be practiced. The pith of the boddhisattva's answer was this:

> Here, O Shariputra, form is emptiness and the very emptiness is form; emptiness does not differ from form, form does not differ from emptiness; whatever is form, that is emptiness, whatever is emptiness, that is form, the same is true of feelings, perceptions, impulses, and consciousness.

> *He is ... the Outward and the Inward*   (57:3)

> All things within the One's solitude lie;
> In its veil, harp and flute raise up their cry.
> The Outward and Inward are all there is;
> Outside of flask and cup, there is no wine.
>
> (Bidil)

The Ineffable and the conceivable are not different in essence. The difference between them is not objective but subjective. Phenomena are not merely empty, or ephemeral in their own-being. They are emptiness itself. They are the Unconditioned in the guise of the conditioned.

> *All things perish except His Face* (28:88)

and still

> *Whithersoever you turn, there is the Face of God*
> (2:115)

> Who is here and what is here?
> "Who" and "what" are one, my dear;
> The vast universal is
> The minute particular.
>
> (Ibn 'Arabi)

As the ocean churns out innumerable waves, the Formless appears in innumerable forms. Such is the overflowing plenitude of emptiness. "The Unconditioned does not exist without the conditioned and the conditioned does not take form without the Unconditioned," observes Jami.

> In separation I saw union concealed;
> Now in union, separation is revealed.
>
> (Abu'l-Futuh)

In this way the world is perpetually dissolved and recreated. Most, however *are in uncertainty as to the new Creation.*

Creation is always a new Creation,
Though it appears to be of long duration.

(Shabistari)

The Friend of God was known to begin his prayer each morning with the words, "O God, this is a new creation!" He Who Has Thus Gone observed, "When the heaps arise, decay and die, O monk, every moment you are born, decay and die."

The world is renewed with each moment's issuance,
While we go on our way, wholly oblivious.
Life comes ever anew, like the flow of a stream,
Yet bodies appear to us as continuous.

(Rumi)

Just as the earth stands in a new relation to the sun and is illuminated anew every moment, in the same way the universe of conditioned things stands in a new relation to its inner ground and is manifested anew every moment. Meanwhile, in its ineffable emptiness the Unconditioned perdures changelessly.

Avalokiteshvara declared:

In emptiness . . . there is no decay and death. There is no suffering, no origination, no stopping, no path. There is no cognition, no attainment and no non-attainment.

Ahmad Chishti and Abu Sa'id Mu'allim were once deep in argument over whether the seeker or the sought should be considered superior. When they asked 'Abd Allah Ansari to settle the matter, he pronounced, "There is no seeker, no sought, no information, no inquiry, no separation, no demarcation, and God is all in all!" Wonderstruck, Abu Sa'id threw off his patched robe with loud exclamations while Chishti fell at Ansari's feet.

To bring the perfection of wisdom within easier reach, Avalokiteshvara offered forth these words for recitation:

> Gone, gone, gone beyond,
> Gone altogether beyond,
> O what an awakening,
>   all hail!

He Who Has Thus Gone then rose from his meditation and commended the wise bodhisattva, while the inhabitants of earth and the heavens rejoiced.

WAVE THREE

Magian Wine

The faith of Zoroaster and the way of the qalandar
Should be made, now and then, the provision of the
traveler.

—Sana'i

I will gird my loins after the Magian custom;
Why? For the very reason that I am a Muslim.

—Khayyam

Stain your prayer mat with wine if the Magus instructs,
For he's not uninformed of the Code of Conduct.

—Hafiz

It is said in the Book, And messengers We have
already told thee of before and messengers We
have not told thee of. *And it is said,* We have sent
no messenger save with the tongue of his people.
*Therefore, among the Iranian people there must be
a prophet, and that is Zoroaster.*

—Bahram bin Farhad

ACCORDING TO Shahab ad-Din Yahya Suhravar-
di (d. 1191), the Master of Illumination, the mystical
legacy of the antediluvian Egyptian prophet Hermes reached Persia in remote times and was kept
alive there by a series of spiritual luminaries, among
whom Suhravardi names the priest-kings Kayumars,
Faridun, and Kay Khusraw; the prophet Zoroaster,
and the sages Jamasp, Frashustar, and Buzurgmihr.

89

Through this chain of transmission the "leaven of the ancients" was passed down to the Sufis Abu Yazid Bistami, Husayn ibn Mansur Hallaj, and Abu'l-Hasan Kharaqani (d. 1033).

Suhravardi explains that his own science of lights, set forth in *Hikmat al-ishraq* (*The Wisdom of Illumination*) and other works, represents a philosophical revival of the symbolic teachings of these legendary figures. At the same time, he is quick to clarify that the "Oriental doctrine of light and darkness" that he follows is of a purely monotheistic character, and therefore not to be confused with interpretations of the ancient Persian religion that deny God's fundamental unity.

In addition to the symbolism of light and darkness, Suhravardi draws upon a number of Zoroastrian motifs in his writings. Chief among these is the angelology of the Zend Avesta, which Suhravardi incorporates creatively in his cosmological system. Suhravardi's cosmology envisions a chain of lights descending from the supreme Light of Lights and successively giving rise to the celestial and terrestrial spheres by process of emanation. Within this shimmering cascade, the Zoroastrian archangel Bahman (Vohuman) features as the First Light produced by the Light of Lights. Four other Zoroastrian archangels appear, together with the Qur'anic Gabriel, as "Victorious Archetypes of Light" responsible for governing their own sublunar exemplars. These are Murdad (Amurdad), who governs plants; Khurdad (Hordad), who oversees waters; Urdibihisht (Ardawahisht), who regulates fires; and Isfandarmuz (Spandarmad), who administers the earth. Finally, Suhravardi conceives of the Avestan *fravashis*, or spiritual principles, as "Regent Lights" tasked with moving the spheres or serving as guardians over minerals, plants, animals, or human beings. Among these is Prince Hurakhsh, the angel of the sun.

Suhravardi was executed on charges of heresy by order of Saladin (r. 1174–93) at the height of the Third Crusade. The shaykh's ideas lived on, however, through his writings, which came to permeate philosophical and mystical circles in the Persian, Indian, and the Ottoman world.

At the court of Akbar, the emperor's chief secretary, Abu'l-Fazl 'Allami (d. 1602), tended a perpetual flame brought from Iran and wove Illuminationist themes into his monumental court chronicle, *Akbarnama*. Describing the ceremony of lights that Akbar observed daily before sunset, Abu'l-Fazl wrote: "Every flame is derived from that fountain of divine light (the sun), and bears the impression of its holy essence. If light and fire did not exist, we would be destitute of food and medicines; the power of sight would be of no avail to the eyes. The fire of the sun is the torch of God's sovereignty."

Akbar's interest in Zoroastrianism prompted him to extend an invitation to the Zoroastrian mystic Azar Kayvan (d. 1618), a native of the Iranian province of Fars. Averse to political entanglements, Azar Kayvan sent the emperor one of his works and excused himself from coming in person. In time, however, Azar Kayvan was drawn to migrate to India, where Akbar's cosmopolitanism provided an attractive aegis for his circle. He settled in Patna, the ancient capital of the Buddhist emperor Ashoka (r. c. 265–38 BCE).

The lineage attributed to Azar Kayvan reaches back to the legendary priest-kings of the Pishdadi and Kayani empires. He is said to have spent his early life in meditative seclusion in the ruined city of Istakhr. During this period "the eminent sages of Greece, India, and Persia appeared to him in dreams and entrusted him with all aspects of spiritual philosophy." In later years he emerged from solitude but remained reclusive. A diverse group of disciples gathered around him, amongst which were Zoroastrians, Muslims, two Jews, a Portuguese Christian, and a Brahmin.

Azar Kayvan's disciples variously described themselves as Yazdaniyan (worshipers of God), Sipasiyan (grateful ones), Azar Hushangiyan (followers of the pre-Zoroastrian prophet-king Hushang, identified with Idris, or Enoch) and Gushasbiyan. The latter term is explained as a Persian rendering of the word *Ishraqiyun*, referring to proponents of Suhravardi's Sufi philosophy of Illumination. Azar Kayvan was hailed as the "King of Peripatetic and Illuminationist Philosophers."

Azar Kayvan's disciples authored a number of works, including, it seems, the mysterious *Dasatir*, a product of visionary encounters with ancient Persian prophets, composed in a "heavenly" language of which no other examples exist. Azar Kayvan himself left behind only a single composition, a string of rhymed couplets in four sections (called *gushasbs*, "illuminations") describing his mystical experiences. The sage's disciple Khuda-jui (d. 1630–31), a native of Herat, penned a commentary and circulated the work under the title *Jam-i Kay Khusraw* (*The Cup of Kay Khusraw*) in honor of Azar Kayvan's son and successor, Kay Khusraw Isfandiyar.

The first illumination concerns experiences described as "visions" (*ruya*). Azar Kayvan begins by explaining how he set out upon the path of the ancients. After tempering the humors of his body, he adopted an impartial attitude toward all articles of belief, withdrew into silence, lodged himself in a dark and narrow recess, fasted, kept vigil, and engaged in the continuous remembrance of God. For Sufis, the primary *zikr*, or practice of divine remembrance, is *La ilaha illa'Llah*, which means in Arabic, "no god but God." Azar Kayvan taught his disciples to recite *Nist hasti magar Yazdan*, which means in Persian, "no existence but God."

Azar Kayvan's initial vision was not pleasant. He saw a crimson veil marked at its center by a dot suggestive of a clot of black blood. A satanic fire flared in his abdomen and chest. He felt a wave of panic, but persevered in remembrance and was at last delivered of the ordeal. In further visions he traversed inner landscapes corresponding to the four elements. Walking, swimming, and flying, he made his way through multicolored fires, gleaming rivers and seas, bracing skies, and earthen streets and dwellings. A light glimmered before him, taking the successive forms of lightning, a lamp, a moon facing his forehead, a sun rising from his chest, a circular spring of prismatic lights, a constellation of stars, and, at last, a conjunction of sunlight and moonlight. This last appearance, explains Khuda-jui, signifies "the spirit of the heart."

There followed a sequence of unveilings in which the seven organs of spiritual perception, known in Sufism as *lata'if* (subtleties), were unveiled in the hermit's inner being. The first of these subtleties revealed itself to be tainted by the lower self. A dark light, turning blue, boasted, "Where is a lord like me?" The second subtlety likewise appeared blue, but resembled sunlight reflected from a pool of water shimmering on a wall. Crimson light accompanied the opening of the third organ, the heart, and Azar Kayvan's flesh became luminous. With the unveiling of the *sirr*, or "secret," a translucent white light appeared, radiating happiness. Next dawned a yellow light that flashed to the right and left and then struck the sage's eyes. Later there came a terrifying black light, which Khuda-jui identifies as the Holy Spirit. Azar Kayvan trembled and fell unconscious. A green light subsequently appeared above his head, resplendent with countless veils. He witnessed an indescribable vision of beauty and was annihilated and revived in God. "That light slayed me; I was no more myself. Everyone said to me, 'you are God.'"

The remaining three illuminations in *The Cup of Kay Khusraw* describe Azar Kayvan's ascensions through the celestial spheres in states of absence (*ghayb*), sobriety (*sahv*), and dispossession (*khala'*). The planets feature in these narratives as angelic Intelligences holding court in their respective spheres. As Azar Kayvan progresses toward the uppermost reaches of existence, he is brought before each of them in succession. Theologians and scholars clad in green surround the Moon. Mercury reigns in a blue world attended by astrologers, philosophers, and physicians. Venus, whose world is white, presides over a court populated by ladies, artists, and craftsmen. In the yellow world of the Sun princes and nobles wait upon the king. Soldiers in red encircle Mars. Jupiter's blue world is a haven for scholars and scribes, while the black light of Saturn attracts Sufis, sages, and soothsayers. Above the planetary spheres lies the heaven of fixed stars, above which looms the Sphere of Spheres. Beyond this, everything is absorbed into God. "Science finds the self, in this state, to be the ocean of the atoms of existent things," observes Khuda-jui.

Read in concert with the philosophical meditations of his disciples, Azar Kayvan's vivid account of his visions and ascensions represents an important elaboration of the Illuminationist tradition. It has been observed that, "the Zoroastrian heritage, piously transmitted and copied through the centuries, never experienced any renewal comparable to the Suhravardian reorientation." It may be added that in giving life to a vibrant school of Zoroastrian Sufism, Azar Kayvan duly returned the favor.

DROP ONE

*The will of
the Lord
is the law
of righteousness*

The Ahunvar

ENDLESS LIGHT emanates from Ohrmazd, who is supreme in omniscience and beneficence. This omniscience and beneficence is called "revelation."

God is the light of the heavens and the earth (24:35)

"Everything is His light," says Muhammad Ghazali, the Proof of Islam.

Opposite the world-illuminating light that ceaselessly radiates from Ohrmazd is the abyss of nonbeing. Here dwells Ahriman, the Destructive Spirit. Light and darkness are undoubtedly contraries, but by no means are they equal opposites. Ohrmazd's benevolent revelation will flourish forever, while Ahriman's existence is the nonexistence of a shadow. "Ahriman never existed and does not exist," agree the magi.

And to whomsoever God assigns no light, no light
has he (24:40)

The Bundahishn narrates that when Ahriman sprang up from the abyss and saw the splendor of the endless light, he quickly retreated and set about fashioning an army of darkness. Ohrmazd invited Ahriman to aid the good creation, but the Destructive Spirit refused, and war was ordained between good and evil. Then Ohrmazd uttered the twenty-one words of the mantra Ahunvar, and Ahriman was laid low for three thousand years.

> *We hurl the truth against falsehood and it prevails*
> *over it*   (21:18)

The Ahunvar, "seed of seeds," begins: "The will of the Lord is the law of righteousness."

The law brought by the prophets is the way of life that accords with the Creator's will. It serves two purposes. First, it maintains the order of the world, enabling people to live in harmony. Second, it establishes the human being in the station of servitude and in this way manifests the majesty of God's Lordship. "Of all things," says Zadsparam, high priest of Sirkan, "that is proper which is something declared as the will of Ohrmazd."

> *We set thee upon an open way*   (45:18)

The Law is a broad road. Beyond it is the Path, which is narrower and steeper. If the Law is learning, the Path is burning. The destination of the Path is Reality. The realization of Reality leads to Wisdom, but that realization does not spell the end of the Law. Reality and the Law are related as heart and body are related. "Matter is animated by the heart, and the house of the heart is matter," observes Sharaf ad-Din Yahya, the Shaykh of Manayr.

In his *Mirror for Mystics*, the martyr Mas'ud Bakk gives another analogy. The Law is a mirror and the Path is polish. Unless it is polished, the mirror will not achieve its end. That end is to reveal the face of beauty, which is Reality.

The Ahunvar continues: "The gifts of the Good Mind to the deeds done in this world for Mazda."

Revelation first came to the prophet Zoroaster while he was wading in the river Daiti. The archangel Vohuman, the Good Mind, appeared to him in the form of a colossal figure robed in light. Vohuman called Zoroaster to follow him and brought him to an assembly of pure spirits where Ohrmazd presided in the presence of His six Powers: Good Mind, Perfect Existence, Desirable Reign, Holy Wisdom, Integrity, and Immortality. When Zoroaster inquired concerning perfection, Ohrmazd answered, "The first perfection is good thoughts, the second good words, and the third good deeds."

Every species on earth has its heavenly archetype, and the archetype of humanity is the Good Mind, known to Jews, Christians, and Muslims as Gabriel. The Good Mind bestows on humanity the gifts of knowledge, confirmation, life, and virtue. These guiding rays illuminate the path that leads to the Abode of Song, the path of thoughts, words, and deeds done for Mazda.

Zadsparam says, "Whoever shall do what is the will of Ohrmazd, his reward and recompense are his own; and he who shall not do that which is the will of Ohrmazd, the punishment at the bridge owing to it is his own."

Adurbad son of Mahraspand says, "I have never done good to anyone in essential matters, nor has any one done evil to me in essential matters, for each of us does the essential things to himself."

Whoso does righteousness, it is to his own gain,
and whoso does evil, it is to his own loss (41:46)

Across the bridge—called *chinvat* by the Persians, *sirat* by the Arabs—is the Abode of Song. Beneath it is the Fire.

Son, if you'd like to know the ego's shape,
Read the tale of hell and its seven gates.
(Rumi)

A dervish once prayed, "O Lord, have mercy on the wicked, since You have already had mercy on the good by creating them good."

Heaven is love's orchard, love's prison is the blaze;
Here is love's effulgence, there love's fiery haze.
(Fayz)

Evildoers will fall into the Fire and suffer the sting of their deeds. Yet even in the Fire the mercy of the Most Merciful is palpable. *Surely God forgives sins altogether.* The Greatest Shaykh observes, "When mercy enfolds you in the Fire, you will surely find that which you suffer sweet."

"In neither world will you behold the sight
Of a place that is deprived of My light."
(Zartusht Bahram)

Yet how much better to have no dealings with the blaze! Then when the soul steps onto the bridge, hell below will call out, "Pass over, true believer, for your light has extinguished my fire."

They have their wage, and their light (57:19)

And who are those happy souls whose light is bright enough to quell the heat of Gehenna? The Succor of the Poor says, "Whoever would be safe from the torment of that day should perform the service regarded by God as the ultimate service: to answer the cries of the oppressed, to meet the needs of the needy, and to fill the stomachs of the hungry."

The Ahunvar concludes: "He who relieves the poor makes Ahura king."

To speak candidly, the generous one is God's friend;
Generosity's the way of 'Ali, King of Men.

(Sa'di)

Faithful worshipers and staunch servants of the One are invariably of generous heart and quick to extend a helping hand. "The sovereignty of Ohrmazd increases that which is for the poor, and adversity is removed," observes Zadsparam.

"The food of the poor is My food, and the drink of the poor is My drink," said the divine Voice to 'Abd al-Qadir Jilani, the Sublime Defender.

DROP TWO

*The satisfaction
of the angels
is the joy
of the body
of good people*

Angels and Adversaries

THE CELESTIAL SPHERES teem with archangels, angels, planetary intelligences, and luminous spirits beyond count who live and move and have their being in the glow of Ohrmazd's endless light, *each swimming in a sky.*

> In each sphere and star I saw a spirit,
> Each aswim between proximate spirits.
>
> (Azar Kayvan)

In the heavens nearest to the earth are angels whose bodies are of mixed light and darkness. Higher up, existence is the light and nonbeing is the shadow in the bodies of the angels. In still more sublime altitudes angels derive their substance from the radiance of the Universal Soul and the lights of the Footstool. Higher still loom luminous intelligences in whom the lights of the Footstool and the effusions of the Throne are mingled. Highest of all are the archangels called the Near Ones and Protectors, whom God creates and sustains from the effulgence of the Holy Spirit and the resplendent lights of the Throne.

To Him the angels and the spirit mount up (70:4)

Ranged against the angels who dispense light on creation is a horde of devils intent on spoiling whatever is good and true. The victory of the angels is

107

ordained; the whole of history must at last culminate in the purest mercy. And yet, for now, the forces of light and darkness are locked in fierce contention, and the front line of the battle is the human body.

The Messenger said, "The devil flows in the veins of Adam's descendents."

Strictly speaking, devils do not exist. They are mere shadows, phantoms of the night. But that is precisely what makes them so pernicious. "A thing that does not exist is that by which the soul becomes wicked," say the magi.

When Ahriman is evicted from every human body, the evil horde will be driven from the world. The dispelling of evil is the first of the two purposes of human existence asserted by the magi. The second is that men and women should serve on earth as witnesses of Ohrmazd.

"My Companions are stars," thus spoke the Prophet,
"Lamps on the path and devil-smiting comets."
(Rumi)

Devils are unseated by the arrival of angels. When Akoman, the Evil Mind, lurks in a person's body, a virtue is hard to conceive. But when the Good Mind takes up residence, a sin is difficult to imagine. And what establishes the Good Mind in the body? In a word, joy.

With clear wine in my glass and my sweetheart so
near,
In the whole of existence I've no one to fear.
(Sharaf)

Joy attracts the angels, and the pleasure of the angels in turn increases the body's natural joy. "The satisfaction of the angels is the joy of the body of good people," say the magi. Conversely, when the body succumbs to distress, the imps perceive an opportunity. Therefore the magi say, "It is necessary to keep one's body in joy and hold one's hand back from doing harm."

> Send out, Lord I pray, Love's battalion
> To crush this treacherous rebellion.
>
> (Imdad)

Love and friendship are formidable sources of joy. By means of the sweetness of gentle fellow feeling and good company, every kind of demon is dismissible. "The love of people is freedom from sin," say the magi.

> It's no labor to me, but pure grace from above—
> It's all pleasure and ease, all affection and love.
>
> (Qadiri)

The Messenger declared: "When divine light expands the breast, the mind is elevated, the bereft are soothed, enemies become friends, distractedness turns to heartfulness, the tablecloth of subsistence spreads out, the rug of annihilation rolls up, the door of sorrow's hermitage is barred, and the gate of union's garden is flung open." In this way the dark army is put to rout and the angels attain victory.

> *He brings them forth from the shadows into the light*
> (2:257)

DROP THREE

O fire of the wise Lord!
May you come close to us
with the joy
of the Most Joyful One

Fire

FIRES VISIBLE and invisible pervade the universe. The source of their radiance is Ohrmazd's Throne, the Endless Light. The magi enumerate five species of fire. The first, "Of High Benefit," blazes in the presence of Ohrmazd. The second, "Loving the Good," resides in the bodies of humans and animals. The third, "The Most Joyful," burns in plants. The fourth, "The Swiftest," flashes in lightning. The fifth, "The Holiest," is enshrined in fire temples. Among holy fires, three are remembered as most venerable: Adur Burzenmihr in Parthia, Adur Farnbag in Fars, and Adur Gushnasp in Media.

> If it's not a shrine to fire, to the breast the heart's
>   a shame;
> The heart in turn bemoans the breath that fails
>   to scatter flames.
>
> (Ghalib)

The traveler on the Path will sooner or later discover fire. Khuda-jui observes, "The fires that appear to the traveler are numerous—to wit, the fires of reality, love, remembrance, passion, and anger, the fire of human desires, and so forth—and it is difficult for all but the perfect to discriminate between them."

Before attaining purer lights the seeker must traverse the dark fires that haunt the benighted recesses of the

113

self. These gloomy flames generate considerable heat but produce little light. Distress signals their arrival. Khuda-jui remarks, "When the traveler on the path of spiritual discipline progresses, he first sees a veil of light resembling a discolored fire. The atmosphere takes on a crimson cast and against this background appears a point resembling black blood."

The antidote to this terror is the remembrance of God. "When a man extinguishes a fire it is a sin; but sometimes when a man extinguishes a fire, it is good," say the magi.

When the dark residues are purged, the body begins to disclose its secrets. In the tailbone, belly, left breast, right breast, chest, forehead, and crown lights are kindled.

> If your spirit and body are illuminated,
> One to another they will be assimilated.
>
> ('Attar)

The lights that descend on the traveler in the first stretches of the Path are called *awqat*, moments of presence. The Sufi is known as a son or daughter of the moment. Sa'd ad-Din Kashgari observes, "Whoever is in one place is everywhere, and whoever is everywhere is nowhere."

> If there is knowledge it's the knowledge that
>   presence sustains,
> But concealed within a veil, as necessity ordains.
>
> (Baqi)

Sometimes the flashes are soothing; other times they strike with a jolt. Various colors appear, each linked to a particular organ of subtle perception. At times

an outer event sparks an inner state. Riding a gallop-
ing horse, moving in a clamorous crowd, witnessing
a scene of war, and similar experiences sometimes
induce gleams and rays. Listening to music at a spiritual soiree deepens the pleasure these flashes bring.

> I saw numerous fires of every possible hue,
> Fires visible to no one except men like statues.
>
> (Azar Kayvan)

God Most High says, *It is He who shows you the
lightning, for fear and hope, and produces the heavy
clouds.* Lightning here alludes to the flashing moments that descend on the novice. The Master of
Illumination, Suhravardi, explains that the fear that
comes from these flashes is the fear of their leaving,
and the hope is the hope that they will remain.

At a later stage the lights do linger on. The heavy
clouds of continuing illumination are called Sakina.

The tranquil fire of Sakina signifies the ascendancy
in the soul of the victorious rays that rain down from
the stars and their spirits. "Glorious is your Revealer
and Illuminator, who pours down the lights that confer
on you the state of eternity!" declares the *Dasatir*.

> A wave of His ocean of light this way flows,
> Crashing through space, above and below.
>
> (Jamman)

The magi name this astral coronation *khurra*, the
Light of Glory. Its recipient becomes an object of the
love and veneration that is due to the angels.

> *He walks in a light from his Lord* (39:22)

The Messenger said, "If God loves a servant, he calls
to Gabriel: 'God loves so-and-so, so love him.' Then

Gabriel loves him and calls to the denizens of heaven: 'God loves so-and-so, so love him.' Then the denizens of heaven love him. Accordingly he is entrusted with the approval of the people of the earth."

The Zend Avesta tells of a lineage of bearers of the Light of Glory, many of them priest-kings — Hushang, Tahmuras, Jamshid, Faridun, the Kayanians, the prophet Zoroaster, and the expected Saoshyant. The tyrant Zahhak tried to seize the khurra, but it cannot be forcibly seized. Nor does it always remain in the possession of the one who attains it. When Jamshid grew boastful, it flew from him in the shape of a bird.

> The days of King Jamshid now grew dim
> As the Light of Glory drained from him.
> (Firdawsi)

When the Light of Glory endures and guides the traveler through ascending spheres, a further station is attained. This is called dispossession. In a body of fire and light the mystic rises through the heavens.

Khuda-jui explains, "The power of detachment reaches such a degree in some of the perfect ones that they are able to separate themselves from their bodies whenever they wish, so that their bodies become like shirts that they take off to put on again at another time. When they detach themselves they join the sublime lights and contemplate the realities contained in them."

> I cast off my body as though it were a coat,
> And conned the starry book that heaven's Author
> wrote.
> (Azar Kayvan)

116

Beyond dispossession is the station of absorption in God. The Messenger said, "Love is fire. When it befalls the heart it burns away all but the beloved."

> Whoosh! and my spirit was consumed by flames,
> Kindled by a fire from another plane.
>
> (Qutb-i Din)

Najm ad-Din Kubra once fell passionately in love with a young woman in a village beside the Nile. As he smoldered day after day, neglecting food and drink, his sighs became flames.

> If a burning sigh from my chest is driven,
> Its flag will fly above the dome of heaven.
>
> (Mu'in)

Then a marvel occurred. Whenever the flame of his breath leapt up into the sky, a celestial flame descended to meet it. Where the two flames met, a presence transpired. This, he realized, was his heavenly witness. In the language of the Avesta, it was his *fravashi*.

Fervent love always meets with a glowing answer in the heavens, even when its object is a mortal human being. As the saying goes, "the phenomenal is a bridge to the Real." The Greatest Shaykh declares, "It is He who manifests to the gaze of every lover in every beloved."

When a lovesick moth plunges into a candle's flickering flame, only the flame survives the tryst. Love unites lover with beloved by obliterating the seeker in the Sought. The forgetting of oneself, and even of forgetting, is called "absorption in absorption."

> As our hearts and souls were but veils in the end,
> We burned them both up for the sake of the Friend.
>
> ('Attar)

To abandon the self is a sacrifice, but the moth's immolation wins the kiss of fire, and there is no higher joy than this. Hence the fire priests pray, "O fire of the Wise Lord! May you come close to us with the joy of the most joyful one."

Our Lord, perfect for us our light   (66:8)

DROP FOUR

May we be the ones
who will make
this world splendid

The Living Earth

"MAY WE BE the ones who will make this world splendid." With these words Zoroaster pressed a reverent appeal to Ohrmazd, invoking in the same breath the holy archangels *encircling about the Throne proclaiming the praise of their Lord.*

Zoroaster's knowledge of the archangels sprang from close acquaintance. After the audience in which he was brought face to face with Ohrmazd, the divine Being, the prophet was summoned to the presences of the six archangels one by one.

Zoroaster encountered Vohuman, the protector of the animal kingdom, on a mountain of two peaks divided by a gushing cataract. Bearing witness were animals of many kinds, feathered, finned, and furred. The assembled creatures confessed their faith in the religion of Ohrmazd, and Vohuman conferred on Zoroaster the custodianship of the animal kingdom.

No creature is there crawling on the earth, no bird flying with its wings, but they are nations like unto yourselves (6:38)

"Whoever is kind to God's creatures is kind to himself," said the Messenger.

He will certainly incur God's displeasure
Who takes the life of a four-legged creature.
(Zartusht Bahram)

121

Ardawahisht, the governor of fire in all of its forms, appeared to Zoroaster at the banks of the Tojan river. Amidst a throng of fire elementals, Ardawahisht instructed the prophet in the maintenance of holy fires.

He knows all creation, who has made for you out
of the green tree fire (3:30)

> That light is one of God's own lights,
> Blazing before you, burning bright.
>
> (Zartusht Bahram)

Shahrivar, the archetype of metals, next showed himself amidst a congregation of metal spirits. His instructions concerned the preservation and proper use of various metals and the chivalric code pertaining to swords and other metal weapons.

Spandarmad, whose province is the earth, received Zoroaster at a mountainside spring. Into the prophet's charge she placed the care of the earth.

> I hereby proclaim the Creator's decree:
> Thou shalt always preserve the earth's purity.
>
> (Zartusht Bahram)

On the same mountain Zoroaster beheld a vision of Hordad, the tutelary archangel of waters. Spirits of rivers and seas attended him as he received the Immortal's benediction and instruction in the guardianship of water.

And we sent down out of heaven water (31:10)

> You must convey this truth to one and all:
> Water is the body's élan vital.
>
> (Zartusht Bahram)

Finally, on the bank of the mighty Daiti river, sur-rounded by a company of plant spirits, Zoroaster was admitted to an audience with Amurdad, the pre-server of the vegetal kingdom. She duly taught him how to care for and propitiate the various plants of the world.

What, have they not regarded the earth, how many there-in We have caused to grow of every generous kind? (26:7)

> To man and beast alike, plants give satisfaction;
> To cause their destruction's an ungodly action.
> (Zartusht Bahram)

Powerful protectors of the natural world though they are, the archangels have their enemies. These are Ahriman's deputies: Akoman, the evil genius; Andar, the tempter; Savar, the agent of misgovernment; Naiki-yas, the fomenter of discontent; Taprev, the poisoner of plants and animals; and Zairik, the manufacturer of poisons. To preserve Ohrmazd's creation from the depredations of its despoilers, the chevalier must stand guard over nature's purity with vigilant rever-ence for the living spirit in everything.

Animals should be slaughtered only as a matter of necessity—so decrees the *Book of a Hundred Gates*. Mubad Hushyar asserts that no animal was ever slain during the golden age over which Kayumars and Siyamak serenely reigned.

Once 'Ali, the Lion of God accidentally stepped on an ant. Seeing what he had done, he was overcome with grief. In a dream the Messenger admonished him to walk more carefully. Ants are constantly engaged in the praise of God. *Nothing is, that does not proclaim His praise.* The Lion shook with sorrow, but:

> "Be happy," said the Messenger, "for all shall be
>   forgiven;
> The ant has sought God's pardon for you at the
>   Court of Heaven."
>
> ('Attar)

Plants likewise belong to the beneficent creation of Ohrmazd. For every flower in the world there is an angel. White jasmine belongs to Vohuman, sweet marjoram is of Ardawahisht, royal basil pertains to Shahrivar, musk flower is in the keeping of Spandarmad, lily belongs to Hordad, and kamba is Amurdad's.

In fact, the very ground from which herbs, trees, and flowers spring is holy.

> In tulip and rose only some are revealed;
> How many faces in the earth dwell concealed?
>
> (Ghalib)

Mountains and rivers exist for the purpose of vivifying the world. Life flows not only in the veins of animals and plants; it circulates equally in the primal elements of creation. "To fire, air, water, and earth were assigned four angels," declares the *Dasatir*.

> To please their Maker the four elements strive;
> Though dead to our lights, in God's eyes they're alive.
>
> (Rumi)

"Do not curse the wind, for it derives from the breath of the All-Merciful," counsels the Messenger.

> Whoever cherishes the elements
> and has kindness for the earth's ruminants,

For such a soul the path is laid open
from hell to Eternity's luminance.

(Zartusht Bahram)

One day the whole world will be healed and made radiantly splendid. In anticipation of that day, here and now it is the duty and pleasure of Ohrmazd's worshipers to defend creation against every kind of pollution and degradation.

And the Earth shall shine with the light of its Lord
(39:69)

WAVE FOUR

The Staff of Moses

I have heard that if one boards Noah's ark and takes
hold of Moses's staff, one will attain salvation.
                    —*Shahab ad-Din Yahya Suhravardi*

As for the family of Moses and Aaron,
Regard them as not of the earth, but of heaven.
                                        —*Sana'i*

Because of you, I love the Jews so well,
I've practically become a Jew myself.
                              —Asrar at-tawhid

SUFISM TRACES its origins to the dawn of history.
Shaykh Sharaf ad-Din Manayri (d. 1381) identifies
Adam as the first Sufi. The shaykh observes, "The
method of Sufism is ancient and was the practice of
the prophets and the righteous." Hazrat Inayat Khan
concurs: "Traces of Sufism are to be found in all peri-
ods of history, but mostly during the age of Hebrew
prophets and ecstatics, who themselves were Sufis."

The Book of Exodus records Yahweh's promise to
make of Abraham "a great nation" (12:2). Hierohis-
tory holds that from Ishmael, son of Abraham and
Hagar, came the Arabs; while from Isaac, son of
Abraham and Sara, came the Jews. The latter line gave
rise to Moses and Jesus, and the religions of Judaism
and Christianity. The former produced Muhammad,

and through him the religion of Islam. The Qur'an instructs believers to proclaim faith in what was revealed to Abraham, Ishmael, Isaac, Jacob, the Tribes, Moses, Jesus, and Muhammad, without distinction.

Certain early Sufis of Islam drank deeply at the wells of Jewish tradition. As a result, Sufi literature abounds in the rabbinical lore of the prophets, known by the term *Isra'iliyat*. Over time, however, the arrow of influence underwent a reversal as a substantial Jewish Sufi movement arose, built largely on the principles of Islamic Sufism.

The first major theorist of Judaized Sufism was the jurist Bahya ibn Paquda (d. c. 1090), who lived in Saragossa during the twilight of Jewish Spain's Golden Age. Ibn Paquda is remembered chiefly for his Judeo-Arabic manual of piety, *Kitab al-hidaya ila fara'id al-qulub* (*Guide to the Duties of Hearts*), which became a popular classic in its Hebrew translation. In *The Duties of Hearts*, Ibn Paquda sets forth a detailed program of spiritual purification anchored in the love of God. While the Bible and Talmud serve as his authoritative touchstones, the author concedes, "I quote also the saints and sages of other nations whose words have come down to us." The Sufis are prominent among these saints and sages; *The Duties of Hearts* draws liberally on Abu Talib Makki's (d. 996) *Qut al-qulub* (*Nourishment of Hearts*) and the works of Abu 'Abd Allah Harith Muhasibi (d. 857).

Ibn Paquda's contemporary Moses Maimonides (Moshe ben Maymun, d. 1204) migrated from Spain to North Africa, where he eventually became physician to Saladin in Fustat, Egypt. Maimonides's magnum opus *Dalalat al-ha'irin* (*The Guide of the Perplexed*), though written in the mode of the Peripatetic school of Islamic philosophy, contains esoteric undertones. It was natural, therefore, for his son and successor, Abraham Maimonides (Avraham Maymuni, d. 1237), to give his father's work a mystical reading. Together with an eminent rabbi known as Abraham ha-Hasid (d. 1223), Abraham Maimonides is credited with popularizing a North African school of pietism (*Hasidut*) that Paul Fenton aptly names "the Jewish Sufi movement."

Abraham Maimonides recognized the Sufis as lineal descendents of the biblical prophets and urged fellow Jews to follow their example. He pointed to the custom of bestowing patched robes on disciples as an example of Sufism's fidelity to the traditions of the prophets. Inspired by the Sufis, the Egyptian Hasidim adopted such practices as ablution, prostration, kneeling, lifting up the palms in supplication, weeping, keeping vigils and fasts, solitude, and the recitation of divine names.

Abraham Maimonides had two sons. The first, David (d. 1300), succeeded his father as leader (*nagid*) of the Egyptian Jews, while the second, 'Obadyah (d. 1265), attained renown as a sage of the Sufi mold. 'Obadyah is best remembered for his *Treatise of the Pool*, which describes the human heart as a pool that must be made pure to receive the living waters that flow from the House of God.

At the same time that Sufi Hasidism was flourishing in Egypt, Kabbalah was flowering in Spain. Among its principal exponents was Abraham Abu'l-'Afiya (d. c. 1295), whose youthful peregrinations in the East likely exposed him to Sufism. Abu'l-'Afiya's "ecstatic

Kabbalah" involved meditative techniques that bear close resemblance to Sufi practices of breath control and invocation. Definite Sufi motifs are observable in the works of two rabbis who appear to have belonged to Abu'l-'Afiya's school, Rabbi Nathan and Isaac of Acre.

Arguably the most unusual personality to occupy the crossroads of Judaism and Sufism was Mir Muhammad Sa'id Sarmad (d. 1660). Born into an Armenian rabbinical family in Kashan, Sarmad received a traditional Jewish education. He later converted to Islam and studied philosophy in Iran under the direction of Mulla Sadra (d. 1571–72) and Mir Findiriski (d. 1640). Afterward he traveled to India where, at a soiree of poetry in Sindh, he met a young Hindu named Abhay Chand and was inspired with a deep Platonic love. Abhay Chand became his disciple and learned the Torah and Psalms from him. For his part, Sarmad seems to have derived a keen interest in Hinduism from Abhay Chand, since he playfully wrote:

> Sarmad! Fame was yours, and what fine aplomb,
> When you quit disbelief and joined Islam;
> Now whatever on earth has made you become
> An ardent devotee of Lakhshman and Ram?

Abhay Chand likewise identified with Hinduism, Judaism, Islam, and in fact all faiths. He wrote:

> I am a follower of scripture, a monk, a deacon;
> I am an Israelite rabbi, a Muslim, a heathen.

Sarmad and Abhay Chand lived by turns in Lahore, Hyderabad, and Delhi, attracting pupils and admirers wherever they went. In Hyderabad Abhay Chand supplied the author of the *Dabistan-i mazahib* (*School of Sects*) with a Persian translation of the beginning of the Book of Genesis, corrected by Sarmad.

In Delhi Sarmad received initiation and authorization in the Chishti Order of Sufism from the hand of Shaykh Abu'l-Qasim Sabzavari (d. 1655), popularly known as Hare Bhare Shah. Hare Bhare Shah's ecumenism is described in these terms: "He extended respect to the great ones of all paths and religions. For this reason a large crowd of Sufis, qalandars, abstracted dervishes, yogis, sannyasins, perfect ones, imperfect ones—in short, all manner of worshipers of God—would gather at his threshold."

Sarmad also became a confidant of the Mughal crown prince Dara Shikuh. Dara Shikuh once sent Sarmad a letter posing pointed questions concerning the nature of divine Will. Sarmad replied simply, "My dear friend! Whatever I have read I have forgotten—except the recollection of the Beloved, which I keep repeating."

Dara Shikuh was executed by order of Awrangzib in 1659, and Sarmad was put to death not long after. The primary charge against him concerned his habit of going naked like a sannyasin, a practice for which Sarmad claimed the authority of no less a figure than the prophet Isaiah.

In martyrdom Sarmad became a second Hallaj, fulfilling a prophecy contained in one of his quatrains:

> By means of love They brought my name low,
> They made me drunk and made my wits go.
> My nakedness was dust on His path,
> That too has been chopped off with a blow.

To this day the shrine of Sarmad stands before the Great Mosque of Delhi, a bright red monument to a free spirit in whose mind and heart Judaism and Islam were inseparably fused in the love of the Friend.

DROP ONE

Say to the Israelites,
"'Ehyeh has sent me to you"

Exodus

THE BOOK OF EXODUS chronicles the journey of the Israelites from occidental exile to freedom and gnosis under the guidance of Moses, the "master of prophets" of the Torah. Signs and wonders leap from its pages.

Though Joseph won honor in Egypt, his descendents were in time reduced to abject slavery. The Israelites enriched Egypt by their toil, but when they "multiplied and grew very vast" their overlords became fearful. Pharoah finally decreed that all Israelite boys be thrown in the river.

Miriam, who is called "Wisdom," placed her infant brother Moses in an ark of bulrushes and left it among the reeds on the shore of the Nile. The Greatest Shaykh tells of how the spirits of all the drowned boys rose up in Moses. The basket was his humanity and the river was the learning he was to gain through the life of the body. In the basket with Moses was the tranquility of Sakina.

Pharoah's daughter discovered the little ark and, peering within, saw "a lad weeping." Gabriel had just then struck a blow at him to smooth the path of destiny. "Once he cries, all evil decrees of the world are annulled," remarks Rabbi Yehudah. The princess' heart melted and she carried the child to the palace.

> Moses and Pharaoh are both within you,
> Find them in yourself is what you must do.
>
> (Rumi)

Raised under Pharoah's protection, Moses learned "all the wisdom of the Egyptians." Then he "went out to his brothers and saw their burden." One day, witnessing a taskmaster assailing a slave, Moses killed him and was driven to flee Egypt. To all eyes he appeared stricken with fear, but something else was at work in the inner recesses of his mind. Love for deliverance was the cause of Moses's flight just as love is the root cause of every impulse—so says the Greatest Shaykh.

In Midian, Moses's gallantry shone brightly and he gained the good opinion of Zipporah, daughter of the priest Jethro, known also as Shu'ayb. Moses and Zipporah were married, and Moses took to tending Jethro's flocks.

At Mount Horeb a revelation came upon the prince-turned-shepherd. "The Lord's messenger appeared to him in a flame from the midst of the bush, and he saw, and look, the bush was burning with fire and the bush was not consumed." As the fire was with the stunted thorn bush, so was God with Israel in its suffering.

A voice bade Moses remove his sandals and approach, declaring, "Moses, *I am God, the Lord of All Being.*"

> Follow the path till like He of the Rod,
> You reach the place where you hear *I am God.*
>
> (Shabistari)

Moses placed his hand on his breast. The hand blanched.

Show your white hand, we pray, O Highness,
Put nights to flight with new dawn's brightness.

(Rumi)

The voice promised the deliverance of the Israelites from Egypt and enjoined Moses to confront Pharaoh.

Come down, O Moses, from your lofty mountain
    fastness,
Dispense revelation to the Pharaoh of Sadness.

(Baqi)

Moses asked by what name he should make God known. The voice answered, "'Ehyeh-'Asher-'Ehyeh, I-Will-Be-Who-I-Will-Be. . . . Say to the Israelites, ''Ehyeh has sent me to you.' "This makes it clear that He is existent not through existence," says the Rambam.

Yahweh alone exists absolutely. All else depends for its existence on Yahweh. Philo comments, "Those who come after Him do not exist in the sense of true being, but are merely by reason of appearances said to exist."

Kalim Allah, the Shaykh of Jahanabad, observes: "The Greatest Name is, in Arabic, O Living, O Eternal; in Syrian, I-Will-Be-Who-I-Will-Be; and, in Persian, O Hope of the Hopeful and Helper of the Helpless."

Though he was, as he put it, "heavy-mouthed and heavy-tongued," Moses was charged with bringing the message of I-Will-Be-Who-I-Will-Be to Pharaoh. Moses was, and is, Speech. He descended Mount Horeb as the Speaker with God.

With his brother Aaron, the Speaker confronted Pharoah with God's command that the Israelites be set free. Pharaoh answered, "Who is the Lord, that I should heed His voice and send off Israel?" He threatened,

139

If thou takest a god other than me, I shall surely make you one of the imprisoned.

The Greatest Shaykh observes, "God in the rank of Pharaoh in outer form held sway over the rank in which Moses appeared in that assembly." Hence, at that moment, Yahweh's will, represented by Pharoah, appeared opposed to Yahweh's wish, represented by the Speaker.

The Martyr of Baghdad comments, "Pharaoh said, *I know not that you have any God but me,* at a time when one who could distinguish between the true and the untrue was unknown among his people. And I say: If you do not know Him, then know His trace; and I am that trace; and I am the Truth, for truly I have not ceased to abide with the Truth!"

Sahl Tustari said, in a similar vein, "The self has a secret that God has not divulged except by the tongue of Pharaoh when he said, *I am your Lord, the Most High.*" But the Shaykh of Rum sees all the difference in the world between the exclamations of Pharaoh and the Martyr of Baghdad:

> Mansur's "I" was a mercy, indeed that is clear;
> Pharaoh's "I" was a curse—mark the difference, my
> dear!
>
> (Rumi)

Pharaoh demanded a sign. *So he cast his staff; and behold, it was a serpent manifest.*

> Moses is religion; repentance is his cane;
> Pharaoh is the ego that must be faced and slain.
>
> (Sana'i)

But Pharaoh remained obstinate, and so the plagues came. Egypt was laid waste. The Israelites departed "and the Egyptians pursued them and overtook them encamped by the sea." The sea opened a path for the fleers and crashed over the heads of the pursuers. He who had drowned the firstborn of Israel sank under the waves.

In the wilderness manna and quails sustained the wandering Israelites. After a spell, the Speaker was summoned to Sinai. For thirty days and nights he fasted and kept vigil. So doing, he was sanctified. God then added ten days to the term, to dissolve the Speaker's sanctity and establish him in the pure station of servanthood. Hence a retreat is undertaken for forty days.

Abu 'Abd Allah Ramli advises, "Make solitude your companion, hunger your food, and intimate prayers your speech. Then either you will die or you will reach God." The principles of seclusion are recitation, purification, lowering the eyes, little speech, little sleep, and little food. Avraham Maymuni confirms that the earliest Hebrew sages secluded themselves in caves, and adds, "The Sufis of Islam likewise practice solitude in dark places"

Overtaken with longing, the Speaker cried out, "Show me, pray, Your glory."

> Show me Your Face in a bolt from the blue;
> Like Moses I've begged so long to see You.
>
> (Amir)

The answer came: *Thou shalt not see me; but behold the mountain—if it stays fast in its place, then thou shalt see Me.* "For no human can see Me and live."

> Before the crag of Being if you call *Arini!*
> Your voice will reecho as *Lan tarani.*
>
> (Shabistari)

The mountain crumbled, and the Speaker swooned. When he awoke he repented and declared himself the first of believers. Not seeing, he had seen. "If you are not, you will see Him," said the Messenger.

> Who could have seen Him? For that oneness is
>   exclusive;
> Had He any two-ness, He'd not be so elusive.
>
>   (Ghalib)

Only Yahweh beholds Yahweh's essence. A creature, as a creature, may witness no more than Yahweh's ways. So asserts the Rambam. But Moses was effaced in his creaturehood, and the Lord, so to speak, "honored him as God." So attests Yeshu'a ben El'azar ben Sira.

Illuminated by the glories of the Face, the Speaker attained the mantle of light worn in Eden by Adam and Eve. His face shone with an overwhelming brilliance.

> Mount Sinai started dancing when it saw the
>   Speaker's light;
> It became a perfect Sufi and turned from wrong
>   to right.
>
>   (Rumi)

To protect those who looked at him from blindness, Yahweh instructed the Speaker to veil his face.

> "If with that robe you cover your face,
> Covered by its veil, the sun won't blaze."
>
>   ('Attar)

Descending from the mountain with the Commandments of Yahweh, the Speaker found the Israelites occupied with the worship of a golden calf. "Moses's wrath flared," but he was moved to beg forgiveness for his people.

The Israelites resumed their migration through the wilderness. A drought struck, and for seven years crops everywhere withered. The Speaker prayed for rain, but I-Will-Be-Who-I-Will-Be answered that the petition of a certain Burkh was wanted. An African dervish named Burkh was at last found and convinced to pray. He badgered the Lord, saying, "What is this that You're doing? Is this an example of Your gentleness?" As he pressed his complaint, rain began to fall. Before the day was out the Israelites were up to their knees in rainwater. The Speaker was taken aback by Burkh's audacity, but Yahweh declared, "Burkh makes Me laugh three times a day."

It once happened that the Speaker came across a shepherd stooped in prayer. In ardent tones, the herdsman urged his wish to comb the Lord's hair, to wash the Lord's clothes, and to serve the Lord a draught of goat milk. The Speaker upbraided the man for his presumption. But then revelation came. I-Will-Be-Who-I-Will-Be made it plain that the shepherd's prayer was as it should be.

> I have assigned a way of living to each;
> To each I've appointed a manner of speech.
>
> (Rumi)

Deepened in understanding, Moses pursued the retreating shepherd and took back his admonition, saying,

> Do not take pains to polish your words;
> What your heart desires, let it be heard!
>
> (Rumi)

The Speaker traveled to the *meeting of the two seas* and found there the green guide Khizr, who possessed *knowledge proceeding from Us.* Khizr agreed to instruct the Speaker in the secrets of gnosis on the condition that he would ask no questions. But the Speaker could not contain his puzzlement when Khizr scuttled a ship and killed a boy. In truth, the "ship" was mortal humanity and the "boy" was vain fancy. When Khizr rebuilt a crumbling wall and the Speaker questioned him for the third time, the guide announced their parting. The "wall" was the soul at peace containing the hidden treasure. The treasure was meant to stay hidden.

> If you'd have immortal peace, then you mustn't
>   mix with men;
> Like the Green One live instead, hidden from the
>   public ken.
>
> (Ghalib)

But the Speaker was duty bound to deliver his people. For forty years the Israelites wandered in the wilderness. Then, at last, the Promised Land came into sight. The Speaker, however, was not ordained to cross the Jordan River. His mission had reached its end. The legacy of prophecy would continue in Israel. "But no prophet again arose in Israel like Moses, whom the Lord knew face to face."

DROP TWO

Sing Him a new song,
play deftly
with joyous shouts

Ascent in Song

ONCE, IN the wilderness, the Speaker went out to find water for his people. Yahweh instructed him to strike a certain rock with his staff. "And water will come out from it and the people will drink." *And there gushed forth from it twelve fountains; all the people knew now their drinking place.* Each fountain, as it flowed, produced a different tune. From these various melodies came the twelve maqams of Eastern music. Yahweh instructed, "*Ya Musa, sqi!*"—"O Moses, give them to drink!" This, it is said, is the origin of the word *musiqi*: music.

> And from Your stream of delights You give them to drink. (Psalm 36:9)

A malevolent djinn troubled the mind of Saul, the first king of Israel. The cure was to listen to his young page David sing and play the lyre. When Saul died in battle, David was acclaimed king. But he became more than a ruler; he became a prophet. From the tongue of David, the Vicar of God, flowed the Psalms.

"God has not sent a prophet except with a beautiful voice," said the Messenger. The Vicar's voice was legendary for its beauty. When he sang Yahweh's praises at dawn and dusk, birds flocked to him and the mountains lifted their voices in exaltation. *O*

147

you mountains, echo God's praises with Him, and you birds!

> The mountain with David was now moved to sing;
> Both crooned drunkenly of their love for the King.
> (Rumi)

It was the custom of the Vicar to keep a harp suspended over his bed while he slept. When midnight came, the north wind would play on its strings. Then the Vicar would awaken and study the Torah until dawn, the hour of hymnody:

> Acclaim the Lord with the lyre,
> With the ten-stringed lute hymn to Him.
> Sing Him a new song,
> Play deftly with joyous shouts.
> (Psalm 33:2–3)

> O strummer of love's lute, a song if you would,
> A melody, please, of the Prophet Da'ud.
> (Jamman)

In intimate converse with Yahweh, the Vicar once exclaimed, "How can I thank You when my very thankfulness is a blessing from You?" The divine Voice answered, "Now you have thanked Me."

Animals and plants too have their joyous shouts of praise. Once, they say, the Vicar grew proud, seeing what a fine musician he was. At that moment a frog crossed his path and croaked, "I recite more songs and praises than you."

> *Nothing is, that does not proclaim His praise,*
> *but you do not understand their extolling* (17:44)

After the Vicar, his son Solomon sang Yahweh's praises. Solomon's songs numbered one thousand

and five. "And no human being has ever ascended in song like Solomon," says Rabbi Yose. In the Song of Songs, which is Solomon's, the entire Torah is contained. "The whole world is not worth the day on which the Song of Songs was given to Israel," says Rabbi Akiva.

The creator of music is the Creator. In the time before time, when God summoned forth the spirits of Adam's progeny and asked, *Am I not your Lord*, God's voice was pure song and the rite of audition was ordained.

God intimated to the Sublime Defender, 'Abd al-Qadir Jilani: "I saw all of the spirits dancing in their bodies since My saying *Am I not your Lord*, until the Day of Resurrection." Behind its screen of dust, every soul dances with abandon to the music of the voice of the Most High.

> I don't know where it was, that midnight
>   convocation;
> All around they danced the dance of immolation.
>
> (Khusraw)

Hymns rang out from Solomon's Temple where four thousand musicians played instruments specially designed by the Vicar. Yusuf Chishti says, "My friend, there are discoveries in audition not to be found in a hundred years of ordinary worship."

> In the religion of love, music is union;
> Sometimes it's the question, sometimes
>   the solution.
>
> (Mas'ud)

Some profess that music is prohibited on religious grounds. The Folk of the Way answer that it is prohibited only to those who cannot digest its nourishment. Audition is for the possessor of a hearing heart.

> Music's detractor is more stubborn than a mule;
> To know God you must know beauty—that is the
> rule.
>
> ('Inayat)

The Proof of Islam, Muhammad Ghazali, writes that banning music makes as little sense as forbidding people to listen to the trills of nightingales. The fire of a secret lies hidden in the stone of the heart. To bring forth that fire, flint and steel are needed. That is what music and singing are.

When the Messenger communicated the secrets of the Path to the Lion of God, he instructed him to reveal them to no one. For forty days the Lion struggled to contain what he had heard. At last, near to bursting, he flew to the desert and lowered his head in a well. Safe from all hearing, he spoke the secrets and found peace. In the days that followed a reed sprang up in the well. A shepherd came, cut it, pierced holes it, and made a flute. When he played on it, people thronged to hear him. They wept and swooned at the beauty of his melodies. Even the camels of the Bedouins were moved to ecstasy. When the Messenger was informed of the shepherd, he called for him. The shepherd played for the Messenger, and his companions fell into raptures. The Messenger said, "These songs are a commentary on the secrets which I told to 'Ali in seclusion."

> Infinite Thou, and infinite Thy ways,
> Therefore the soul expands to sing Thy praise.
>
> (Ibn Gabirol)

DROP THREE

The dark and the light
will be one

A David Psalm

PSALM ONE HUNDRED and thirty-nine tells of God's omniscience, omnipresence, and limitless luminescence.

The psalm sings, "You fathom my thoughts from afar."

Yahweh sees the unseen as well as the seen, disincarnate thoughts as well as embodied actions. *God knows the thoughts in the breasts.* Everything is transparent before the divine Sight.

The psalm sings, "From behind and in front You shaped me, and You set Your palm upon me."

We are artifacts of the Artisan. Our form, inward and outward, answers the description of the Holy One. "God created the human in His image."

> God created us in His very own image;
> A form modeled on His—that is our privilege.
>
> (Rumi)

We have honored the children of Adam (17:70)

The masculine and the feminine aspects of reality reside equally in the One. The Kabbalists hold that the first-created human being was both male and female. Yirmeyah son of El'azar observes, "When the blessed Holy One created Adam, He created him androgynous, as is said, 'Male and female He created

153

them.'" "Behind and in front" refers, it is said, to the female and male faces of Adam-and-Eve.

> *O mankind, We have created you male and female,*
> *and appointed you races and tribes, that you may*
> *know one another*   (14:13)

God said, according to a narration: "I have created mates for things that My unity may be evidenced." In the union of two, the One is remembered.

> When man and woman are as one, the remaining
>   one is You;
> When both are made to disappear, the prevailing
>   one is You.
>
> (Rumi)

The psalm sings, "Darkness itself will not darken You, and the night will light up like the day; the dark and the light will be one."

Spiritual light is uncovered in the depths of physical darkness. When the eyes see only darkness, the soul's eyes perceive brilliance. During vigils in the night, the gnostic is wrapped up in shadows. That is when the sun dawns at midnight. Therefore, "night and day are called one."

> Don't sleep, my dear fellow! Stay up through the
>   night;
> Only then will you see the night sun shine bright.
>
> ('Attar)

"Though he walk in darkness and have no light, let him trust in the name of the Lord and rely upon His God," counsels the prophet Isaiah. The descent of God's own light on the gnostic is a more than generous compensation for doing without lamplight.

> My night is the morning sun of Your Face,
> darkness is merely a feature of space.
> People dwell in darkness due to their night,
> while due to Your Face, we bask in the light.
> *(Rawh al-arvah)*

The psalm sings, "The days were fashioned, not one of them did lack."

Are these days the days when every destined soul lived nonexistently in God in the time before time evoked in the revealed words: *Remind thou them of the days of God*?

Only by God's love for the soul was the nonexistent soul made existent. Ahmad Ghazali, the Father of Victory, therefore has good reason to exclaim, "Is it not a sufficient mark of distinction that Adam was God's beloved before he was God's lover? This is no small badge of honor!"

Or are the mentioned days the days in which the universe was created—the days of light and darkness; of water and sky, of earth, sea, and plants; of sun, moon, and stars; of birds and fish; of animals and man; and of Yahweh's holy rest? Those primordial days are "the Lebanon cedars He planted," immense and ancient trees growing out of the soil of wisdom. So great is the light of those days that, could one see it, it would engulf the light of the sun as the sun engulfs the light of the stars.

> We are mere drops of dew, while You are the Sun;
> Should You choose to appear, what will we become?
> *(Amir)*

Or, rather, are the sung-of days the days of the spinning week? On each of these days, says the Greatest

Shaykh, there is a presiding prophet: Enoch on Sunday, Adam on Monday, Aaron and John on Tuesday, Jesus on Wednesday, Moses on Thursday, Joseph on Friday, and Abraham on Saturday. Muhammad, says the shaykh, pervades them all.

All of these days belong to the Ancient of Days. *Every day He is upon some labor.* There is no lack of days because Yahweh is time itself. The Messenger said, "Do not curse time, for God is time."

The psalm sings in closing, "Search me, God, and know my heart, probe me and know my mind. And see if a vexing way be in me, and lead me on the eternal way."

Surely God is witness of everything. Yahweh's awareness of the world and all that it contains is constant. But awareness of that awareness is rare in this world. To pray, "Search me . . . know my heart . . . probe me . . . know my mind," is not to beg for a glance that is absent. It is rather to lift one's gaze to meet the shaft of knowing light that has transfixed every fiber of one's body, heart, and soul for as long as one has lived. That is the light that illuminates and guides the seeker's progress on the way to the eternal goal.

> O Lord, I pray, favor me with a glance;
> In the midst of this gloom, kindle a lamp.
>
> (Hasan)

DROP FOUR

*Where were you
when I founded
the earth?*

Job

ON THE second day of creation, the divine Sakina branched into two manifestations: Hesed on the right and Gevurah on the left. Hesed is mercy, symbolized by water. Gevurah is judgment, symbolized by fire. From Gevurah comes the fiery figure of Satan, the Adversary, the Accuser. "He goes down and incites, then he goes up and accuses, he takes you over and he takes your soul," say the rabbis.

Satan has been called the "Tempter" and the "ego." He has also been called the "Guardian of the Divine Presence" and the "Servant of the Attribute of Force." Since God's writ runs in everything, even the Accuser must be, in the last analysis, God's instrument. *He leads astray whom he will, and guides whom he will.* And even those led astray are at last guided, since *Surely unto God all things come home.*

> I am enamored of mercy and wrath;
> How strange to love both, as much as they clash.
>
> (Rumi)

Job was a man of wealth and honor. One day the angels came before Yahweh, among them the Adversary. The Lord spoke fondly of Job. The Adversary contended that Job was faithful only on account of the favors Yahweh had granted him. "And yet, reach

159

out Your hand, pray, and strike all that he has. Will he not curse You to Your face?" And the Lord allowed the Adversary to test Job.

When Shibli was committed to an asylum, some people came to visit him. He asked who they were. They answered that they were his friends. He at once began to pelt them with stones. As they ran away, he called after them, "Liars! Had you been my friends you would have been patient when I tested you."

Job was left bereft of children and possessions. Yet he remained devout. "You incited Me against him to destroy him for nothing," remonstrated Yahweh in the spirit of Hesed. The Adversary rejoined that a blow to his body would certainly make Job a blasphemer. This test too the Lord allowed. Worms were sent to riddle Job's skin. "And he took a potsherd to scrape himself with, and he was sitting among the ashes."

Though reduced to utter ruin, Job refused to curse Yahweh. *Surely we found him a steadfast man.* He insisted, "Shall we accept good from God too, and evil we shall not accept?"

"This is the belief of Israel: to receive the judgments of Elohim with joy and enjoy His afflictions, His rebuke, and His judgments and to thank Him for all, and bless His name," says Joseph Gikatillah.

Three friends came to console Job. They wept loudly when they saw him, tearing their robes and throwing dust on their heads. They counseled him to accept his trial as retribution for his sins. But Job was not content with their explanation. He wanted to see the Lord face-to-face. "Would that I knew how to find Him, that I might come to where He dwells."

The Proof of Islam explains that there is more to an illness than meets the eye. Secondary causes aside, an illness is "a cord of love" by which God's friends are drawn toward God's presence. Ordeals are especially given to prophets and saints, and those who follow their ways.

Job yearned to plead his case before God. And yet, he knew that God would inevitably overwhelm his contentions. "How can man be right before God?... Who can argue with Him and come out whole?"

The Shaykh of Rum tells of how a gnat once brought a suit against the East Wind at the court of Solomon. After hearing the insect's testimony, Solomon summoned the Wind. The Wind's arrival blasted the gnat away and the case was abruptly concluded.

> At the Court of the Lord, so is it fated,
> When God comes, the inquirer is negated.
>
> (Rumi)

God is not ashamed to strike a similitude even of
a gnat (2:26)

Job called out, *Behold, affliction has visited me, and Thou art the most merciful of the merciful.* He groaned, "My skin turned black upon me, my limbs were scorched by drought. And my lyre has turned into mourning, my flute, a keening sound."

Some say Job's complaint revealed the imperfection of his patience. Abu 'Ali Daqqaq says, "God drew forth these words from Job, namely *affliction has visited me*, to make breathing space for the weak ones of this community."

Others think differently, maintaining that Job's complaint spelled no lack of patience. When his state called for silence, he kept silent; when it was incumbent that he cry out, he cried out. When he complained, he complained only to Yahweh.

God is not aloof from hurt; such is plain from the words *those who hurt God and His messenger.* The Greatest Shaykh explains that it hurts God to try a servant who has fallen into forgetfulness. The relief of that hurt comes when the servant complains to God, and in complaining, remembers. "Then," says the Greatest Shaykh, "your need of God, which is your reality, becomes true, and by your beseeching relief from God, God's own hurt is alleviated, because you are His outer form."

> The object of all of that suffering was a sigh;
> With the sigh came deliverance from the Most High.
>
> ('Attar)

From the whirlwind Yahweh thundered, "Where were you when I founded earth? Tell, if you know understanding."

> *I made them not witnesses of the creation of the*
> *heavens and earth* (18:51)

Job answered, "By the ear's rumor I heard of You, and now my eye has seen You. Therefore do I recant, and I repent in dust and ashes." And health and wealth were restored to him.

> Ever modest before God's knowledge, and true to
> the core,
> Job remained as milk and honey throughout all
> that he bore.
>
> (Rumi)

> *So be thou patient with a sweet patience* (70:5)

WAVE FIVE

The Messiah's Breath

It is related that when he heard the sound of a church bell, 'Ali ibn Abi Talib, may God be pleased with him, asked his companions, "Do you know what it says?" They answered, "No." He said, "It says, 'Praise be to God, truly, truly. The Lord endures forever!"

—ar-Risala al-Qushayriya

If with a sign she demands the New Testament,
You would reckon us priests in clerical vestments.

—Ibn 'Arabi

When I was reconciled to Christianity's tenets,
I drank the wine of love and renounced my wonted penance.

—'Attar

Should Venus intone the words of Hafiz perchance,
Do not be surprised if Christ himself joins the dance.

—Hafiz

AS A CHILD, the prophet Muhammad once accompanied his uncle Abu Talib on a trading journey to Syria. In the town of Busra he attracted the attention of a Christian monk named Bahira, who at once recognized in him the signs of his destiny. According to Sufi lore, Bahira had in his keeping a chivalric sash that had come down to him from Jesus himself, who had in turn inherited it from the ancient prophets. Bahira bestowed it on Muhammad and announced

165

his prophetic station. Many years later, when revelation descended on Muhammad, it was the Christian cousin of his wife Khadija, Waraqa ibn Nawfal, who affirmed his experiences and hailed his prophetic mission.

When a group of persecuted companions of Muhammad migrated to Abyssinia, the Christian ruler of that land, called the *negus,* extended his protection over them. Hearing them read the Prophet's revelations, he wept until his beard was wet, and said, "Of a truth, this and what Jesus brought have come from the same niche."

On the day when Muhammad returned victoriously from Medina to Mecca, he ordered that the images inside the Ka'ba be erased. The narrator Azraqi reports, however, that he made an exception: of all of the images, he spared an icon of Jesus and Mary. That picture is said to have remained in the Ka'ba until Umayyad times.

The Qur'an says of the Christians, *Some of them are priests and monks, and they wax not proud.* The early Sufis of Islam met these unassuming followers of Jesus in Egypt, Palestine, and Syria. It is often asserted that the word *sufi* derives from *suf,* meaning "wool," the coarse fabric Sufis donned in harmony with the custom of the Christian ascetics.

The impact of Sufism on Christian spirituality is difficult to gauge in the early period. Beginning in the High Middle Ages, however, Sufism's imprint appears in a number of theological and poetical works produced by Christian authors. The *Kethabha dhe-yauna* (*Book of the Dove*) and *Kethabha dhe-'ithiqon* (*Ethi-*

kon) of the Syrian bishop Gregory Bar Hebraeus (d. 1286) closely follow Muhammad Ghazali's *Ihya' 'ulum ad-din* (*Revival of the Religious Sciences*). The Majorcan polymath Ramon Llull (d. 1316) patterned his celebrated *Llibre d'amic e amat* (*Book of the Lover and the Beloved*) on literary models derived from the Sufi School of Love. Intriguing commonalities exist between Muhyi ad-Din Ibn 'Arabi's (d. 1240) treatment of the Ascension of the prophet Muhammad in his *al-Futuhat al-makkiya* (*Meccan Openings*) and Dante Alighieri's (d. 1321) description of his own otherworldly journey in the *Divine Comedy*. Sufi symbols saturate the writings of the great Spanish mystics Saint John of the Cross (d. 1591) and Saint Theresa of Avila (d. 1582). And in recent times, Pope Francis included a saying of the Sufi 'Ali Khawas in his encyclical letter *Laudato si'*.

Ibn 'Arabi explains that among those Muslim Sufis who may be counted as God's friends, some are in the mold of Moses, others in the mold of Jesus, and still others are in the mold of Muhammad. The outstanding example of a Christic (*'isawi*) mystic is the Sufi martyr Husayn ibn Mansur Hallaj (d. 922). Hallaj's controversial pronouncement, "I am the truth," seems to echo Jesus's dictum, "I am the way, the truth and the life." According to legend, Hallaj visited the Holy Sepulcher in Jerusalem at night and miraculously lit up four hundred lamps. Other miracles credited to Hallaj bear resemblance to events in the Gospels. Most strikingly, Hallaj's collected poems contain the line, "I will die in the religion of the cross." Such in a sense was his fate: following trial and imprisonment, like Jesus, Hallaj was crucified.

Other Sufis may also be named. Abu Bakr Wasiti (d. after 932), a disciple of Hallaj, is said to have been an *'isawi* saint like his teacher. 'Ayn al-Quzat Hamadani (d. 1131), who revered Hallaj, was put to death at the age of thirty-three—the same age as Jesus. Waris 'Ali Shah (d. 1905) of Dewa Sharif, India, and Shaykh Ahmad 'Alawi (d. 1934) of Mostaganem, Algeria, are two examples of modern saints who were perceived in a Christic light. Hazrat Inayat Khan was asked on several occasions whether he was Christ himself.

The crucifixion of Jesus is a subject of historical disagreement between Christians and Muslims. For Christians, the crucifixion and resurrection of Jesus is a central article of faith. When the Qur'an mentions the crucifixion it says, *They did not slay him, neither crucified him, only a likeness of that was shown to them.* Muslim exegetes have generally understood this to mean that Jesus was not crucified. Some, however, read the verse mystically, asserting that while Jesus's humanity (*nasut*) died of the cross, his divinity (*lahut*) suffered neither death nor crucifixion. This was evidently the understanding of Hallaj. In the throes of his crucifixion he reportedly recited, *They did not slay him.*

Another subject of dispute between Christians and Muslims is the doctrine of the Trinity. Christians and Muslims share the belief that Jesus was born to Mary without a physical father. While the Gospels invoke Jesus as the "Son of God," the Qur'an declares that *God has not begotten, and has not been begotten.* For exoteric interpreters the doctrinal divide on this point seemed insuperable, but Sufis see differently.

Ibn 'Arabi wrote in a verse, "My Beloved is three although He is one, even as the (three) Persons (of the Trinity) are made one Person in essence." By way of commentary, he explained that "number does not beget multiplicity in the divine substance," adding that the cardinal divine names in the Qur'an are three: Allah, ar-Rahman, and ar-Rabb.

Concerning the essence (*adh-dhat*), Ibn 'Arabi's follower 'Abd al-Karim Jili wrote, "If you say that it is One, you are right; or if you say that it is Two, it is in fact Two. Or if you say, 'No, it is Three,' you are right, for that is the real nature of man." Jili maintained that the secret of Lordship was revealed to Jesus and Muhammad alike, but whereas Muhammad transmitted it only esoterically, Jesus disclosed it openly, with the result that misunderstandings arose when Christians took Jesus's allegorical expressions literally.

The Persian poet Mahmud Shabistari, who likewise belonged to the school of Ibn 'Arabi, devoted the last pages of his influential *Garden of Mystery* to an esoteric appreciation of Christianity. Shabistari identifies the goal of Christianity as *tajrid*, a term used by Hallaj to designate the state of mystical abstraction. He refers to God as the "Sublime Father," using the Aramaic word *Abba*, and says:

> Therefore Jesus said at the moment he ascended,
> "I am in harmony with my Father in heaven."
>
> (Shabistari)

Mention should also be made of the later poet Hatif Isfahani (d. 1783). One of the stanzas of his celebrated poem of five stanzas (*tarji'-band*) describes an imagined conversation with a Christian "ravisher of hearts." Hatif writes:

> In a church I said to a Christian belle,
> "Captor of my spirit, please listen well.
> The tip of every one of my hairs
> Is attached to the Christian sash you wear;
> But why don't you walk on unity's path?
> How long must the Trinity hold you back?
> How can you designate God, who is one,
> As the Holy Ghost and Father and Son?"
> Her sweet lips parted and she answered me.
> With lips spilling laughter deliciously.
> "If you realized unity's enigma
> You'd be less quick to brand me with stigma.
> Upon three mirrors the Ancient of Days
> Hurled from His Countenance shimmering rays.
> Silk remains silk and does not become three
> When called taffeta, samite, and pongee."
> While in this fashion she and I conversed,
> From the church bell a chant suddenly burst:
> "The Lord is one and never were there two
> He is one—*La ilaha illa Hu!*"

Hazrat Inayat Khan's secretary Sirkar van Stolk left an interesting account of a visit the two men made to Rome in 1924. In this vignette, Hazrat Inayat Khan's enthusiasm for the spiritual presence he described as "the living Christ" comes across vividly:

> I had accompanied Murshid to Rome where, one morning during our stay, we heard that the Pontifical High Mass, officiated over by the Pope himself, was to be celebrated in St. Peter's the next day. This is a special Mass held only once every year, and Murshid asked me to try to get tickets

for the occasion. I did try; but after many fruitless efforts was obliged to return to the hotel with the news that tickets had been sold out months before. Murshid did not appear to be as cast down as I by this information; and the following morning, about half an hour before the Mass was due to begin, he asked me to order a carriage.

"It will be impossible for us to get in to the High Mass!" I exclaimed. But Murshid simply repeated his request: "Please order a carriage." I did so, and we set out from the great Piazza in front of St. Peter's; Murshid dressed in his usual simple black cassock. When we arrived, the Square was full of activity and a sense of anticipation. A row of the famous Swiss Guards in their theatrical blue and orange uniforms stood at the foot of the wide steps leading up to the Cathedral. Their job was to turn away anyone arriving without the big white card necessary for admittance.

"You see," I said to Murshid, "Absolutely impossible to get in." Nevertheless, he stepped out of the carriage and asked me to pay off the driver. Slowly he walked towards the morning-coated dignitary checking the cards at the foot of the steps. The latter, the epitome of lordly officialdom, duly asked in Italian for his card. Murshid looked at him, smiling, and firmly, with utmost courtesy, replied, "It is quite alright."

Although he spoke in English, his tone was irresistible. The man moved back, overcome in the presence of this majestic stranger, and let Murshid through. I quickly slipped in behind him, as a sort of shadow; but whereas I had a tremendous desire to hurry up the steps before being ignominiously called back again, Murshid ascended in a completely unruffled, stately manner.

At the head of the steps stood another row of Swiss Guards, and in their midst an even more impressive personage than before, in what appeared to be full evening dress. Again, Murshid was asked for his card; and again, with exactly the same air of courteous authority, he smiled and replied, "It is alright," moving quietly on as he did so. The official, like his counterpart at the foot of the steps, was obviously much awed by Murshid, by his serene appearance and the tone of his voice, and he too, to my utter astonishment, stepped back. We were through.

As we entered the radiant gold and white interior of that marvelous building—the largest Basilica in all Christendom—the choir began to sing in what I can only describe as a heavenly manner, the sound echoing against dome and arches with unearthly beauty. At that moment the Pope was borne in on a golden throne carried by twelve priests. The High Mass had begun.

As the intoning of the Pope, the chanting of the choir and the movement of priests and censers became interwoven in that great festival of worship, the whole atmosphere became charged in the most wonderful way; charged with something mystical and incredibly beautiful. Light streamed through the golden aureole in the little window above the High Altar; gleamed on the marble floor; flickered over the eighty-nine candles which burn day and night round the tomb of St. Peter.

Murshid was going more and more deeply into a state of ecstasy. Rapt and still, he seemed in another world. And then suddenly, as if the words had been wrung from him, he cried, "How wonderful is the power of the living Christ!"

DROP ONE

With God nothing
will prove impossible

Our Lady

ANNA VOWED that if God would give her a son notwithstanding her barrenness, she would entrust the boy to the Temple. A child did come—but a girl! Anna named her Mary and pledged her to service, though hitherto only boys had served at the Temple.

Our Lady was lodged in a sanctuary at the top of a stairway. Summer fruits sustained her in the winter and winter fruits in the summer. *Truly God provisions whomsoever he will without reckoning.*

No one exceeded Our Lady in acts of glorification. Alone, she communed with the Eternal and inhaled eternity's effusions of splendor.

The goal of "true virginity" is the ability to see God, observes Gregory of Nyssa. The Speaker urged the Israelites to prepare for Yahweh's revelation by abstaining from conjugal embraces. "How swift, O virginity, are your wings that reach your Lord," exclaims Ephrem the Syrian.

On a fateful day, a resplendent figure broke in on Our Lady's solitude. It was Gabriel, the Trusty Spirit. He calmed Our Lady's fears and announced that she would bear a *boy most pure.* The Virgin Mary could not contain her astonishment, but the archangel assured her, "With God nothing will prove impossible." Faithful to the marrow, she gave her fiat of assent,

"I am the Lord's servant; as you have spoken, so be it."
And life was breathed into her womb, as life was once
breathed into the clay of the Pure.

> *We breathed into her of Our Spirit*　　　(66:12)

> From Mary's water or Jibril's breath,
> 　　in the form of man, molded in clay,
> The Spirit itself took existence,
> 　　in an essence exempt from hell's sway.
> (Ibn 'Arabi)

Ephrem sings, "The virgin earth gave birth to that
Adam, head of the earth; the Virgin today gave birth
to Adam, head of heaven."

> In this world, that breath was Adam's father
> That made the Virgin Mary a mother.
> (Sana'i)

Some days after Gabriel's call, Our Lady paid a visit to
her kinswoman Elisabeth, wife of the prophet Zechariah.
Elisabeth, the True Turtledove, had meanwhile conceived the child that would become John the Baptist.
When Mary appeared, a sudden lurch of her holy
burden told her that Our Lady's womb contained the
Messiah. "The baby stirred in her womb. Then Elisabeth was filled with the Holy Spirit."

> When I came before you just now,
> The child within me made a bow.
> (Rumi)

At the same moment Jesus, the Spirit of God, bowed
to Saint John in Our Lady's womb, fulfilling the verse,

"Kindness and truth have met, justice and peace have kissed."

Surely Our Lady was the Lord's servant and a saint. Some say she was also a prophet. She is called "Our Lady of Sorrows" in honor of the grace with which she bore seven staggering blows. Her tribulations reached their climax when she witnessed her son's crucifixion.

Though the sight of the crucifixion was terrible to witness, in truth the Spirit's persecutors were powerless to injure his spirit. The Revelation of Peter narrates that the Spirit said to Saint Peter, "The one you see smiling and laughing above the cross is the living Jesus. The one into whose hands and feet they are driving nails is his fleshly part, the substitute for him."

> *They did not slay him, neither crucified him, only*
> *a likeness of that was shown to them* (4:157)

Ruzbihan Baqli explains, "Observe that in reality, when his eye turned to spirit, his form became pure soul and he disappeared from the dust. How could material accidents touch him? Do you not see that when it was finished, Jesus ascended to heaven?"

At the close of her days, Our Lady departed the world in a blaze of glory. The apostles gathered around her. Next the prophets and martyrs arrived. Then came the angels in procession, throng after throng. Finally the Spirit of God appeared. He gently saluted his holy mother and laid his right hand on her eyes. Our Lady asked to become an intercessor for

God's mercy. The Spirit confirmed that it would be so
and led her soul to the mansions of light.

> The holy Mother Mary with the Christ Child
> Bends o'er the world with benedictions sweet;
> And down the ages comes Muhammad's saying
> That heaven is lying at a mother's feet.
>
> ('Inayat)

DROP TWO

*In the beginning
was the Word*

The Word

A VISITOR once came to see the desert father Achillas. Noticing blood dripping from the hermit's mouth, he ventured to inquire what was wrong. Achillas answered, "A brother came and said something that upset me, and I have been brooding over that grievance. I prayed God that he would take it away, and the word turned into blood in my mouth. Look, I have spat it out, and I am now at peace and have forgotten my grievance."

Words are consequential. A good word is a good tree: *its roots are firm, and its branches are in heaven.*

> Wherever generosity's tree takes root,
> Straight to heaven its trunk and branches upshoot.
> (Sa'di)

By the same token, a corrupt word is a corrupt tree: *uprooted from the earth, having no stablishment.*

The Spirit of God said, "Out of your own mouth you will be acquitted; out of your own mouth you will be condemned." A word once spoken will be heard again, for better or for worse.

> Only when you have breathed your last
> Will what was hid be manifest.
> ('Attar)

181

A good word is good for one and all. Saint Paul said, "Speak the truth to each other, for all of us are the parts of one body."

The Spirit passed a group of people who hurled slurs at him. For every evil word they spoke, the Spirit responded with a good word. Saint Peter asked, "Will you answer them with good each time they speak evil?" The Spirit replied, "Each person spends of what he owns."

The Spirit not only owned and spent good words—he was and is a word, *God's own Word*. The Word that God *committed to Mary* came from the time before time. Therefore the Gospel of Saint John declares: "When all things began, the Word already was."

> Because he is the very Word of the Truth,
> Jesus is honored as pure spirit in sooth.

> ('Attar)

The Master of Illumination explains that the primal Word is the Holy Spirit, whose light fills the universe. From the Holy Spirit proceeds a succession of Great Words, celestial intelligences kindled by the glories of the august Face. They are known as *those that outstrip suddenly*. The last of them is Gabriel, who breathes spirit into humankind.

After the Great Words come the middling words. These are the angels that move the heavenly spheres, *those that direct an affair*. The empyrean is abuzz with their discourses.

Lastly come the lesser words, the vibrations of all earthly beings. "Not on bread alone does the human live but on every utterance of the Lord's mouth does the human live," declares the Torah. *When he decrees a thing, He but says to it "Be," and it is.* The lesser words are rays that have tumbled down from the Holy Spirit. These rays are limitless in number, as God says:

> *Though all the trees in the earth were pens, and the sea-seven seas after it to replenish it, yet would the Words of God not be spent* (31:27)

A man who was reputed to be wise came to Anthony of Egypt and inquired how he managed to pass his days without the consolation of books. The saint replied, "My book, sir philosopher, is the nature of created things, and it is always at hand when I wish to read the words of God."

There is no word without breath, no syllable without a vowel. Through the Word of the Messiah an immense gust of spirit flows.

On account of this, while he walked the earth, the Spirit's breath healed the sick and raised the dead. After the crucifixion, the Spirit blew on his disciples, saying, "Receive the Holy Spirit."

> O sweet breeze of Jesus, I pray that all your days
> be blessed,
> For the heart of Hafiz came alive owing to your
> breath.
>
> (Hafiz)

Creation is God's speech. The Breath of Mercy gives vent to God's thoughts. "By the Word of the Lord the heavens were made, / and by the breath of His mouth all their array."

> All is in the Breath, just as light
> Lies within the essence of night.
>
> (Ibn 'Arabi)

As every breath comes from and returns to the One's own Breath, there is no better utterance than a word that ascends with the briskness of a homecoming breeze. "Purity is the translucence of the noetic air, and in the bosom of this air, our nature takes wing," says Isaac of Nineveh.

To Him, good words go up (35:11)

DROP THREE

*There is joy among
the angels of God
over one sinner
that repents*

Purification

"THE WAY OF JESUS, peace be upon him, is to struggle in solitude and not to indulge one's lust," observes the Shaykh of Rum. The soul's victory over sin is not easily won, but with triumph comes joy in the heavens. "There is joy among the angels of God over one sinner that repents," declares the Spirit of God.

As Abba Isaac points out, it is far easier to cure a patient who is aware of his sickness and acquainted with its cause than to cure one who is ignorant of his condition. In view of this, the hesychasts carefully analyzed the common maladies of the soul. Evagrius Ponticus enumerates eight kinds of evil thoughts. They are: gluttony, impurity, avarice, dejection, anger, despondency, vainglory, and pride.

> At every step loom a thousand snares;
> Love's not for the faint of heart, my dear!
>
> ('Ayn al-Quzat)

The first evil thought, gluttony, is the tyranny of an insatiable appetite. When the mind is at the beck and call of the belly, it cannot assist the work of the soul. Compulsive eating dulls the senses and blurs the faculty of inner vision.

> On the feet it is a chain and on the hands a bind;
> The belly is a slave, but not the worshipful kind.
>
> (Sa'di)

"Surely life is more than food," exclaimed the Spirit on the Mount.

The answer to gluttony is moderation and fasting. John of the Ladder is eloquent: "Fasting is the door of compunction, humble sighing, joyful contrition, and end to chatter, an occasion for silence, a custodian of obedience, a lightening of sleep, health of the body, an agent of dispassion, a remission of sins, the gate, indeed, the delight of paradise."

The Shaykh of Bistam agrees: "Hunger is a cloud. When the servant is hungry, wisdom rains down on his heart."

> An untainted inwardness—go bring that forth,
> For the belly can be filled only with earth.
>
> (Sa'di)

> *Surely we will try you with something of fear and*
> *hunger*   (2:155)

The second evil thought, impurity, is the crude sensuality of the endarkened ego. When it rears up, conflict breaks out between the hesychast's lower nature and the guiding light of the spiritual principle within. "That nature sets its desires against the Spirit, while the Spirit fights against it," explains Saint Paul.

> Whoever stirs up lust, devoid of any love,
> Wishes, evidently, to spill his own lifeblood.
>
> (Sa'di)

Avarice, the third evil thought, is obsessive brooding over money and property. It follows from distrust in Providence and discontentment with the simple things of life. Fear of penury is its hallmark. Evagrius observes, "Avarice suggests to the mind a lengthy old age, inability to perform manual labor, famines that are sure to come, sickness that will visit us, the pinch of poverty, the great shame that comes from accepting the necessities of life from others."

The antidote is situating the mind in the present moment. Hence the Spirit preached on the Mount: "Do not be anxious about tomorrow; tomorrow will look after itself."

> Come! Let's forget tomorrow's pain,
> And make the most of today's gain.
>
> (Khayyam)

Kharraz remarks, "Do not occupy your precious time with anything except that which is most precious, and the most precious of things for God's servant is to be occupied between the past and the future."

> Whether you strive, or not, for your sustenance
> It is supplied, regardless, by Providence.
>
> (Sa'di)

Dejection, the fourth evil thought, is sorrow over worldly losses and disappointments. The sadness that brings to mind God is a blessing and a joy, but the sorrow that lingers mournfully over fleeting phantasms is an ailment of the heart.

> The very days of time are aghast
> At the one who sits and grieves the past.
>
> (Khayyam)

Praise belongs to God who has put away all sorrow from us (35:34)

The fifth evil thought, anger, is a violent passion rooted in arrogance, turbulence, and greed. Sooner or later it brings down the one who gives in to it.

> When you blasted hearts in the heat of your rage,
> You became a source of the infernal blaze.
>
> (Rumi)

A man asked the Messenger for advice. The Messenger said, "Do not become angry." The man pressed his request again and again. The Messenger kept giving the same answer: "Do not become angry."

The Spirit admonished on the Mount, "Anyone who nurses anger against his brother must be brought to judgment." Anger too long nursed is anger that outlasts daylight. "Do not let sunset find you still nursing it," urges Saint Paul.

One of the remedies for anger in the hesychast's medicine chest is readiness to accept dishonor. A person who is not concerned with others' opinions is immune to the provocation of insults and false accusations.

> Though the charge of heresy has been leveled at me,
> As I'm drunk, reputation's an irrelevancy.
>
> (Sharaf)

He will remove the rage within their hearts (9:15)

Despondency, the sixth evil thought, is listnessness of body and mind. It makes the hesychast look out the window and pine for another scene. The hermit who cannot throw off the sway of this "noonday demon" is doomed to wander from place to place, never finding peace.

Fortify me, O contentment, with your substance,
For apart from you there's never been abundance.

(Sa'di)

Since despondency is born of distraction, its cure is attention. John of the Ladder observes, "The cat keeps hold of the mouse. The thought of the hesychast keeps hold of his spiritual mouse."

Shibli learned the art of contemplation from a cat. He explained, "Once a cat was sitting in front of a mouse hole in such a way that not a single hair on its body moved. It wasn't even aware of the people around it. The thought entered my mind that if an irrational animal exercises such presence of mind in obtaining its food, why should a human, who is so superior in intellect and gnosis, do less?"

The greed of my despondency was brought at last
    to rest;
My roving hand descended on the object of my
    quest.

(Bidil)

Vainglory and pride, the seventh and eighth evil thoughts, are related but different. Vainglory is the enjoyment of others' regard. Pride is the enjoyment of one's own.

A monk was once seated in an assembly. The demon of vainglory came and sat at his right side, and the demon of pride came and sat at his left. The demon of vainglory poked and prodded him, urging him to talk about his visions and exploits in the desert. He held his tongue. Seeing this, the demon of pride whispered in his ear, "Well done! Well done! You have become great by conquering my shameless mother."

> You fell when you glanced at yourself in pride;
> A curtain was drawn then over your eyes.
>
> (Sharaf)

But fear not, says John of the Ladder: "If pride turned some of the angels into demons, then humility can doubtless make angels out of demons." "To the humble the mysteries are revealed," promises Abba Isaac.

It once happened that, as the Spirit walked out of the desert, he came across a pious hermit. The hermit prostrated in reverence when he saw the Messiah. Meanwhile, a reprobate passed by. This good-for-nothing had passed his years in drunkenness and infamy. Seeing the Spirit and the hermit he was transfixed, as a moth by a flame. A wave of remorse passed over him, and under his breath he implored God's pardon for his sins, weeping copiously. When the hermit observed him, he frowned and shrank back, murmuring, "O Lord, when groups are gathered on the Day of Resurrection, please do not gather him with me!" Hearing this, a revelation came over the Messiah, and he pronounced, "If the worshiper of worship is ashamed to be this man's neighbor in Paradise, say he need have no shame of him on the Day of Resurrection. For this man will be carried to Paradise, while he is carried to the Fire."

> On this threshold, wretchedness and helplessness
> Are better than righteousness and selfishness.
>
> (Sa'di)

"Whoever exalts himself will be humbled, and whoever humbles himself will be exalted," assures the Spirit.

To subdue the demons of gluttony, impurity, avarice, dejection, anger, despondency, vainglory, and pride, repentance is necessary. To repent is to acknowledge one's sins, seek forgiveness, and steer a new course.

> My words and actions were all untoward;
> To You now I flee—Forgive me my Lord!
>
> (Fayz)

The force behind repentance is the longing all creatures feel for the Good. Overhead, a host of angels look on in joy.

> My sins are great, that I know to be true;
> But greater still is the mercy in You.
>
> (Sarmad)

So holy is the forgiveness God bestows on supplicants, Amir ventures to say:

> As my sins arouse the mercy of my Lord,
> Never to sin would be a sin of a sort.

DROP FOUR

*The Kingdom
of God
is within you*

Illumination

WHEN THE hesychast's soul is purged of its vices through repentance and watchfulness the resulting state of grace is called illumination. In the station of illumination the hesychast is wholly given over to the contemplation of God. Contemplation leads at last to the condition of mystic absorption known as perfection.

Perfection is a path of several steps. Bar 'Ibraya enumerates twelve: the baptism of the mind, awareness of distinction, love of recitation, outbursts of tears, love of all humankind, the bright burning of the mind, hearing the angels, mirroring the divine nature, becoming like fire, unification, joy without reason, and ecstatic speech.

The baptism of the mind occurs within the heart. Its precondition is silence. When words fade away, mental constructs likewise subside and the serene mind merges into the spacious heart. Whereas the ordinary workings of the mind are complex and frequently confused, the heart's knowledge is free of convolution. "Spiritual knowledge is simple," says Abba Isaac.

Abraham of Nathpar observes that in the depths of silence the movements of the mind are stirred "solely by Being."

Simple awareness makes the gnostic young again. The Spirit instructed those who aspired to the Kingdom of God to turn around and become like children.

Hierotheos comments, "When the mind has been accounted worthy to ascend above the firmament, it then becomes as a babe that has just been born."

At this juncture the mind becomes conscious of the high estate to which God has raised it, as attested in the primordial pronouncement, *I am setting in the earth a viceroy.* Saint Paul expresses it in this way: "In Christ He chose us before the world was founded, to be dedicated, to be without blemish in His sight, to be full of love."

> We are the kings of the land of oblivion,
> We are the lords of poverty's dominion.
>
> (Sufi)

The Kingdom of God is within you. (Luke 17:21)

The gnostic now takes delight in chanting the verses of scripture at every opportunity. The holy songs of the Vicar are always on the tip of the hesychast's tongue.

Hajji Imdad Allah gives these instructions for the recitation of the Qur'an. Imagine that the tongue of your mouth and the tongue of your heart are reciting together. Do not neglect your heart's recitation. In this way you will attain peace and the presence of God. Now feel that all of the limbs, organs, and hairs of your body are reciting in symphony. Next, conceive that God is reciting with your tongue and listening with your ears. Now go further still and witness that God is the speaker and listener, while you do not exist at all. A single voice rises from all things, and you lose yourself in it.

Not all reciters of the Word reach such depths. But as Gregory the Great says, scripture is a river in which lambs may wade and elephants may swim.

Tears presently begin to well up in the gnostic's eyes unaccountably. Bar 'Ibraya explains, "The fire of love warms the heart and makes tears flow from the eyes."

> Tears keep erupting out of my eyes,
> This inner burning never subsides.
>
> (Raz)

Mas'ud Bakk's tears were said to be so hot, if they fell on someone's hand it was burned.

> To see mystically your eyes must be damp;
> Light only shines when there's oil in the lamp.
>
> (Amir)

The flame in the mystic's heart is love of God and compassion for all of God's creatures. Abba Isaac explains, "It is the heart's burning for the sake of the entire creation, for men, for birds, for animals, for demons, and for every created thing; and at the recollection and sight of them, the eyes of a merciful man pour forth abundant tears."

With this in view, Evagrius instructs, "Pray first for the gift of tears."

> Hot tears and cold sighs I ask of You,
> Paint my lovesick face a pallid hue.
>
> (Siraj)

As tears spill out, the gnostic's love for humanity engulfs the entire world. Distinctions are of no account in this love. The gnostic invokes God's mercy equally on sinners and saints, men and women, and people of all races, nations and religions.

"The Creation is God's family," said the Messenger. The loyal servant of the God accordingly wishes the best for all creatures. In this spirit, the Shaykh of

Bistam prayed, "O Lord, on the Day of Resurrection make my members and limbs so large that they fill the seven levels of hell, so that there is no room for anyone else!" Saint Paul said in a similar vein, "I could even pray to be outcast from Christ myself for the sake of my brethren, my natural kinsfolk."

Love now burns so brightly that all extraneous thoughts are consumed and the gnostic's mind is brought fully out *from the shadows into the light.* The Spirit made allusion to this state when he said, "I have thrown fire upon the world, and look, I am watching it until it blazes."

The source of the light that shines in the hesychast's heart is the radiance of the Good. Gregory of Sinai therefore exclaims, "Our God is fire!" Dionysius the Areopagite explains, "God Himself is really the source of illumination for those who are illuminated, for He is truly and really Light itself."

Dionysius advises the seeker of celestial light to imagine a great shining chain hanging down from heaven to earth. The seeker should seize it with one hand and then the other as though pulling it down. In fact, the chain is not descending; the seeker is ascending, lifted by the starry chain of being.

The Master of Illumination tells of how, in the throes of a vision of cosmic destruction, the priest-king Hermes called out, "Father, rescue me from the enclosure of those who live in the shadow of evil!" The answer came, "Take hold of the cable of rays and climb up to the battlements of the Throne." Hermes climbed up and there, beneath his feet, was a new earth and a new heaven.

When the mind is kindled, the gnostic begins to see without eyes and hear without eyes. The chants of the seraphim now become audible, as they were to the prophet Isaiah.

> Born of breath, we are candles of being;
> Around us spin moths—seraphs, I mean.
>
> (Mas'ud)

The voices of the angelic hosts take the form, not of words, but of "intellectual sounds," or noetic vibrations. As the Shaykh of Jahanabad says, "The entities of the universe are distinguished by different modes of recitation, and every species and genus is occupied with its appointed recitation."

> *All that is in the heavens and the earth magnifies*
> *God*   (59:1)

> When I gave ear to the proclamation of truth,
> I heard everywhere, *La ilaha illa Hu.*
>
> (Fayz)

It happens then that the gnostic, immersed in pure light, takes on the likeness of light, just as a cloud lit up by the sun takes on the semblance of the sun. Hitherto the gnostic wore a distorted aspect, "choked by cares and wealth and pleasures of life." Now, at last, the earthly image reclaims the splendor of its celestial archetype. "Your divine beauty will again shine forth," exclaims Gregory of Nyssa.

As a result of this transfiguration, the gnostic's very body becomes a living flame. "The righteous will shine as brightly as the sun," promises the Spirit.

The desert father Arsenius attained such intense illumination that not only did his spirit glow, his very flesh blazed. One day a monk came to see him in his cell and found him standing in prayer. To the caller's eyes he appeared simply as a flame.

It is said of Muhammad Chishti that he needed no lamp for his nightly studies, but instead read by the light pouring out from under his turban.

When this condition is attained, unification is not far off. In unification, the distance between lover and beloved is reduced to nothing. All supplication and entreaty ends here. Therefore Abba Isaac says, "Prayer is terminated when those insights which are born in the spirit from prayer pass into ecstasy."

> The power of the Most High will overshadow you.
>   (Luke 1:35)

God says of the gnostic in this state, *When I love him, I am his hearing by which he hears, his sight by which he sees, his hand by which he holds, and his foot by which he walks.*

Here is the account of the Shaykh of Bistam:

> "My qualities became the qualities of Lordship,
> my tongue became the tongue of unification,
> and my qualities became: 'He, He, no god but He.'
> Then what was was what it was by His being
> and what may be was what it may be by His being.
> My qualities were the qualities of Lordship,
> my signs were the signs of eternity,
> and my tongue was the tongue of unification."

The state of unification is a bubbling fountain of joy.

> Miserable is the one who is far from the Friend,
> While the one linked with union is happy and
>   content.
>   (Qutb-i Din)

In this state, the gnostic requires no earthly justification to experience transports of the purest happiness. "The mind only knows that it rejoices here, not why it rejoices," observes Bar 'Ibraya.

> What is there in you and me when only He exists?
> Our being is purest nothing, so what explains this
>   bliss?
>
> (Mas'ud)

Now, as Bar 'Ibraya notes, come outbursts of speech, mystical utterances divulging the meanings hidden in God's archbook, the *guarded tablet*. Though frequently paradoxical, these words bring "a blessing to those that hear."

Once the Spirit took the Apostle Thomas aside and said three sayings to him. When his friends later asked Thomas what the Spirit had said, he replied, "If I tell you one of the sayings he spoke to me, you will pick up rocks and stone me, and fire will come from the rocks and consume you."

When the Shaykh of Bistam was in a state of contraction he expressed himself only in sighs, but when a wave of expansion came over him he grew eloquent. Ecstatic confessions would sometimes fly from his tongue. Once he exclaimed, "Glory be to me, how sublime is my stature!" When the state dissipated and his disciples informed him of his outburst, he was mortified. He gave them knives and instructed them to kill him if he spoke like that again. And it happened again. His disciples attempted to apply his instructions, but his body was suddenly as big as the room and as amorphous as water. Then it shrunk down to the size of a sparrow. When his disciples later recounted what had happened, the shaykh said, "Bayazid is this person whom you see. That was not Bayazid."

The friend of God is only sometimes the person you see.

DROP FIVE

*You shall don
your splendid robe*

The Robe of Glory

THE HYMN of the Pearl, which was sung by the Apostle Thomas during his imprisonment in India, tells of the soul's exile in the world and its homecoming in heaven. The protagonist is a prince whose name Thomas does not mention. He is the spiritual principle in everyman.

The hymn begins: "When I was a little child and dwelt in my realm, in my father's house, and was at ease with rich delights of those who nourished me, then from the East, our native land, my parents furnished me and set me out."

The East is the cosmic Orient, the pleroma of pure luminous Intelligences. Before sending him off, the king and queen presented their son with a treasure of precious metals and jewels. More importantly, they revealed a magnificent robe they had prepared for him, promising it would be his when he fulfilled the pact they now inscribed on his heart:

> If you descend to Egypt and retrieve the pearl unique, in the middle of the sea, hard by the hissing serpent, you shall don your splendid robe and your tunic resting on it, and with your brother, our second in command, the heir you shall be in our realm.

We offered the trust to the heavens and the earth
and the mountains, but they refused to carry it
and were afraid of it; and man carried it (33:72)

The prince set out in the company of two expert guides: the Universal Soul and the Universal Intellect. Traveling through Maishan, Babel, and Sarbug, the three voyagers at last reached Egypt, where the prince's guides left him.

Maishan, Babel, and Sarbug must be understood as *arwah*, *ajsam*, and *mithal*, the planes of spirits, astral bodies, and imaginal forms. Egypt is *nasut*, the world of sense impressions and land of spiritual forgetting.

You have seen the form but not what is inside;
Extract the pearl from the shell if you are wise.

(Rumi)

The prince immediately located the undersea lair of the serpent and took up lodgings at a nearby inn. There he kept watch, waiting for the serpent to doze off.

What is the inn? Recall the tale of Sultan Ibrahim and Khizr. One day when Sultan Ibrahim was holding court, a stranger approached his throne. The sultan demanded, "What do you want?" The man answered nonchalantly, "I'm just stopping at this inn." Sultan Ibrahim shouted, "You are mad!" The man asked, "Who owned this palace previously?" Sultan Ibrahim replied, "My father." "And before him?" "My grandfather." "And before him?" "So-and-so." "And before him?" "The father of So-and-so." Now he came to the point: "Isn't this an inn then, where one comes and another goes?" With these words he vanished.

The mortal world is an inn. And what is the serpent? Ibn Sirin says that a snake in a dream symbolizes an enemy. The Messenger said, "Your greatest enemy is between your two sides." The serpent, therefore, is the ego.

> The ego is hell and hell is the dragon;
> Pour oceans on it, still its fire won't slacken.
>
> (Rumi)

At the inn, the prince befriended a fellow countryman from the East. He was wary of the people of Egypt and warned his friend against them. To evade their scrutiny he adopted their style of dress. He also tasted their food. As a result, he suffered a derangement of the mind.

> I forgot I was a royal son, and I served their king.
> The pearl, too, I forgot—the very thing for which
> my parents had sent me out. Through their heavy
> food, I fell into a deep sleep.

The *Pistis Sophia* calls the lethe of the Egypt of the senses "the water of forgetfulness." To drink it is to forget one's heavenly homeland and to be inured to the degradation of exile.

> This world's oblivion runs so deep
> Life's daylight fades while still we sleep
>
> (Amir)

When the king and queen of the East came to learn of their son's plight, they resolved to send him a message. They wrote: "Awake and rise from sleep . . . recall you are a son of kings . . . recall the pearl . . . remember, too, your splendid robe."

Will you not remember? (37:155)

What do you possess and what have you achieved?
What have you fetched from the depths of the sea?
(Rumi)

The letter flew to Egypt in the form of an eagle. When it landed beside the slumbering prince it became all word. Hearing its sibilant rustlings, the prince awoke, kissed it, and read its message. All at once, he remembered everything.

The prince now rose resolutely and confronted the serpent. Chanting his father's name over the monster, he succeeded in lulling it to sleep. The serpent thus subdued, the prince seized the object of his quest.

The pearl that was hidden inside my heart,
You've seized it, my dear, by means of some art.
(Ziya')

The pearl is the spiritual embryo formed in the womb of the heart that is illuminated by the divine presence. Hear what the Shaykh of Rum says about the conception of the Messiah in the bosom of the gnostic:

Against the little soul the Cosmic Soul pressed,
So that a pearl was sent into the soul's breast.
Like the Virgin Mary, due to that caress,
It conceived a Christ Child, beloved and blessed.
(Rumi)

Having obtained the pearl, the prince took off the "vile and filthy clothes" to which he had reconciled himself in Egypt.

> Those who went forth impersonally
> Reached the desert uncovered and free.
> (*Wujud al-'ashiqin*)

The *Gospel of Thomas* records these words of the Spirit: "When you strip without being ashamed and you take your clothes and put them under your feet like little children and trample them, then you will see the child of the living one and you will not be afraid."

> *Thy Lord magnify, Thy robes purify, and defile-*
> *ment flee!* (74:3–5)

The prince was now ready to return home. The letter flew before him and guided him through Sarbug, Babel, and Maishan. As he reached the frontier of the East, his parents' treasurer welcomed him and presented him with his appointed robe and tunic.

The Master of Illumination calls the robe assumed in heaven the "raiment of dawn." What the one who wears it imagines is fulfilled.

> Suddenly, when I confronted it, as if in my mirror,
> the garment seemed like me. I looked at the whole
> of it, complete, and in it faced myself entire, for
> we were two in separation, yet we were also one
> in single form.

The robe was embroidered with jewels and emblazoned with the image of the King of Kings. Gentle murmurs emanated from its folds. As the prince reached out to take it, the robe leapt into his hands. Donning it, he was lifted up to the "gate of peace and adoration."

The prince's father rejoiced at his son's victorious homecoming. "This son of mine was dead and has come back to life; he was lost and is found." Together with his brother, the prince was now heir to the realm of the East. It remained for the king to take his son to the court of the King of Kings to present, as tribute, the pearl.

Many are the meanings enclosed within the sea;
Let others have the bubbles, the pearl is for me.

(Ghani)

WAVE SIX

The Seal of Prophecy

I am the Qur'an's slave, so long as my heart beats,
Mere dust is what I am beneath Muhammad's feet.
                                                    —Rumi

I tell you, Khusraw, love's fire has singed my mantle;
In that night-dark place, Muhammad was the candle.
                                            —Amir Khusraw

IN THE GOSPEL OF JOHN, Jesus says, "I will ask the Father, and He will give you another to be your Advocate (*parakletos*), who will be with you forever —the Spirit of Truth." This prophecy reappears in different terminology in the sixty-first sura of the Qur'an, where Jesus foretells of *a messenger who shall come after me, whose name shall be Ahmad.* A tradition circulated among Sufis says, "I am Ahad beyond the Throne, Ahmad in heaven, Muhammad on earth, and Mahmud on the Night Journey." Hence in Sufism, Ahmad is understood as the celestial name of Muhammad.

The early Christian theologian Origen (d. 253) identified the parakletos as the Holy Spirit. He taught that the same Holy Spirit indwells in all of the biblical prophets. Sufis designate the light common to all prophets as the *Nur-i Muhammadi*, or "Muhammadan Light." They trace this light back to the beginning of time. Shah Muhammad Taqi Niyazi writes:

215

When the divine Essence wished to manifest a thousand years before the appearance of the universe, it kindled a Light capable of manifesting the Master of the World, peace and blessings of God be upon him, and placed it in the Court of Intimacy. After dwelling at length in the divine Intimacy, the Light was given leave from worship and glorification, and with the urgent command 'Be!' it was brought forth as an Emanation in ten parts. From the first the Throne was made, from the second the Tablet, from the third the Pen, and from the fourth, fifth, sixth, seventh, eighth, and ninth, the moon, the sun, heaven, hell, the angels, the earth, and the sky. From the tenth part the Spirit of the Great Medium was created and established on the Throne. The Light occupied the Throne in brilliance for seventy thousand years and the Footstool for five thousand years. Then, hearing the abstract divine command communicated through Gabriel, Michael and Seraphiel, it obeyed the Creator's command and descended to the earth and sought a portion of clay. With the restlessness of ardent love the earth split open and offered up a portion of white clay it had kept in trust. Gabriel brought another portion of white clay from the place that is now the Master's resting place. Leavening the two with the dust of the paradisial fountain of wine called Salsabil, Gabriel prepared the substance of the existential body of the Master, peace and blessings be upon him. Invoking the angelic hierarchies, he declared the joyful tidings, "In this dust is the Beloved of the Lord of all Worlds, the Merciful Interceder, peace and blessings of God be upon him. Before the appearance of Adam his light was the Sun of Truth and now a receptacle has become needed for his light." Then Adam, peace be upon him, said in the language of spirit, "O desired treasure, seat yourself in the ruins of my heart, for I have made it an empty ruin in my longing for you."

Hazrat Inayat Khan refers to the Nur-i Muhammadi as the "Spirit of Guidance." Recognizing this light as the inner spirit of all messengers and prophets, he maintains that Shiva, Buddha, Rama, Krishna, Abraham, Moses, Jesus, Muhammad, and many others, known and unknown to history, were in essence "always one and the same person." In Muhammad, he says, the prophetic mission reached its terminus:

> Each prophet had a mission to prepare the world for the teaching of the next; each one prophesied the coming of the next, and the work was thus continued by all the prophets until Muhammad, the *khatam al-mursalin*, the last messenger of divine wisdom and the seal of the prophets, came on his mission, and in his turn gave the final statement of divine wisdom: "None exists but Allah." . . . This final definition is a clear interpretation of all religions and philosophies in the most apparent form.

Muhammad is credited with a number of miracles, including the Splitting of the Moon and the Night Journey and Ascension, but tradition reveres the revelation of the Qur'an as the greatest of his miracles. Rumi writes, "When you take refuge in God's blest Qur'an; / you mingle with the prophets who have come and gone." He explains, however, that the wisdom of the Qur'an is not forthcoming to all in the same degree. To access the Qur'an's inner truths it is necessary to approach the Book as a devoted groom approaches a bashful bride. Only to the patient and sincere does the Qur'an unveil its treasures.

A'isha said of Muhammad, "His character was the Qur'an." Rumi said further, "Whoever partakes of the light of God becomes the Qur'an." In his capacity as Seal of the Prophets (*khatam an-nabiyin*, 33:40), Muslims acknowledge Muhammad as the last prophet. Sufi theologians add that while the cycle of legislative prophecy (*nubuwwat at-tashri'*) reaches its majestic culmination with Muhammad, inspiration (*nubuwwat al-'amma*, or *walaya*) continues among the friends of God. Hence Hazrat Inayat Khan calls Muhammad the "root of all murshids and the fruit of all prophets." Rumi writes:

> They say that after the Chosen One, peace and blessings be upon him, and the prophets who came before him, peace be upon them, revelation (*wahy*) will not descend on anyone else. Why shouldn't it descend? It does, only it is not called revelation. That is what the Prophet meant when he said, "The believer sees by God's light." When one sees by God's light one sees everything: the first and the last, the absent and the present. How could anything be hidden from God's light? If something is hidden from it, it is not God's light. So the meaning of revelation persists even though it is not called revelation.

The Prophet revealed the injunctions of sacred Law (*shari'a*) to all Muslims. The methods of the mystical Way (*tariqa*), by contrast, he communicated only to those who were prepared to undertake the inner journey with the necessary resolve. First and fore-

218

most of these was his cousin and son-in-law ʿAli ibn Abi Talib. Shaykh Nasir ad-Din Chiragh-i Dihli (d. 1356) relates:

> Once ʿAli, may God ennoble his face, approached the Messenger, peace and blessings be upon him, and said, "O Messenger of God, show me the nearest way to God, the way that is easiest for the worshiper and most preferred by God." He replied, "O ʿAli, adhere to something that I have acquired through revelation." ʿAli asked, "What is that?" He replied, "The remembrance (*zikr*) of Allah." ʿAli asked, "The excellence of remembrance, which all men do, is of this kind?" He replied, "O ʿAli, the Hour of Doomsday will not strike so long as one person on earth says, '*Allah Allah*.'" ʿAli asked, "How should I perform the rite of remembrance?" He replied, "Close your eyes and be still while I say the phrase of remembrance three times and you listen." The Messenger instructed ʿAli in the rite of remembrance in this way. He sat facing the direction of prayer and the Messenger sat beside him facing the direction of prayer. Then the Messenger said three times, "*La ilaha illa' Llah*" (there is no god but God).

The mystics among the Prophet's companions consisted primarily of the "People of the Bench" (*ahl as-suffa*), the devout mendicants who lived in the Prophet's Mosque in Medina. Mention is made of these Sufis avant la lettre in the Qur'anic verse, *And do not drive away those who call upon their Lord at morning and at evening desiring His countenance.* The Prophet said to them, "Be of good cheer, O People of the Bench! Each of you who is content with your present state will be among my friends and companions on the Day of Judgment."

In the last year of his life, at the pool of Khumm, the Prophet famously took 'Ali's hand and proclaimed, "Whoever's master I was, 'Ali is his master." Having received spiritual succession from the Prophet, 'Ali passed it on to Hasan, Husayn, Kumayd bin Ziyad, and Hasan Basri. These masters subsequently took on disciples, who in turn took on their own disciples. In this manner the lineages of Sufism multiplied. The transmission of Sufism continues to the present day in varying manifestations. As a cautionary note, however, it bears recalling that a thousand years ago it was already said, "Today Sufism is a name without a reality, whereas it used to be a reality without a name."

DROP ONE

So remember Me,
and I will remember you

Bearing Witness

THE POLYTHEISTIC Meccans of the Age of Ignorance acknowledged the existence of a Supreme God known by the name "Allah." Allah seemed to them, however, so remote and unapproachable as to have no bearing on their lives. They had recourse therefore to a pantheon of demigods whose likenesses they worshipped in figures of wood and stone.

When the Messenger proclaimed the Message he dispelled the Meccans' illusions. God is neither distant nor indifferent! Allah is the *Outward*, the *Inward*, the *All-Merciful*, and the *All-Compassionate*.

To speak of "gods"—and still more confusedly, to worship them—is to obscure the oneness of the One. God is boundless by every measure, and what has no boundary cannot be multiple. *Were there gods in heaven and earth other than God, they would surely go to ruin.*

Faith in God's oneness develops in three stages. At first, the profession of faith is little more than a formality. The tongue declares God's unity, but the heart is sunk in distraction. God is just a word, forgotten as soon as spoken.

> How long will your tongue remain your only
> means of prayer?
> To pray in such a fashion is to pray to thin air.
> (*Maktubat-i sadi*)

If the believer desires to know God and sets out on the Path, a truer belief will be born. The believer must continuosly remember, *There is no god but God.* These words must be understood to mean, "There is no object of worship but God."

In the first stage of belief, believers are inclined to conceive of God as as powerful advocate. As injured parties seek the representation of a capable attorney-at-law, when there is adversity to be vanquished believers turn to God. Then, when circumstances are restored to stability, forgetfulness returns.

If the believer remembers God day in and day out, patient in misfortune and grateful in prosperity, the second stage will transpire. At this juncture *There is no god but God* comes to mean, "there is no destination but God." The believer is now a traveler on the Path and a witness to the fact that God is the source and goal of everything.

> Beholding Your works is my eyes' daily rite,
> Proclaiming Your praise is my tongue's sole delight.
> (Sana'i)

The traveler on the Path no longer acts like the client of a barrister. What he or she desires from God is not God's puissance so much as God's presence. As Shibli expresses it, "Sufis are infants in the lap of God."

> With certainty they are at ease, and with its
>   spiritual grace,
> Content with a child's contentment when wrapped
>   its mother's embrace.
> (ar-Risala al-Qushayriya)

The profession of faith has moved from the tongue to the heart. The believer is now answering an imperative as old as time: *Remember Me, and I will remember you.*

> *In God's remembrance are at rest the hearts of*
> *those who believe* (13:28)

Remembrance is always mutual. The Father of Victory, Ahmad Ghazali, observes, "If the connection between the lover and beloved is established, it is necessarily fastened on both sides, for it is the prelude to oneness."

> *He is with you wherever you are* (57:4)

To attain the reality of unity, the believer must undergo deeper and deeper self-forgetting in the remembrance of God. *There is no god but God* now comes to mean, "there is no existing thing but God."

> Our only song is of our unmaking;
> We are the sound of our own strings breaking.
> (Ghalib)

Someone asked Sa'd ad-Din Hamuya, "What is God?" He answered, "That which exists is God." The questioner asked, "What is the world?" He answered, "Nothing exists but God."

When the Path to God merges into the Path in God, the third stage of faith materializes. The believer has passed from the *knowledge of certainty* to the *eye of certainty*, and from the *eye of certainty* to the *truth of certainty*. The seeker's soul now reposes in God's hands with the serenity of a body that, having breathed its last, yields completely to the touch of the one who is to perform its final washing. There is no more remembrance in this state—for what is remembrance to the one who is absorbed in the Remembered?

Some compare absorption in God's unity to the disappearance of the stars in the sky when the sun rises. But this is an experience that cannot be adequately described. The divine Voice told the Sublime Defender, "Union is a state that language cannot express."

For the one who lives in God, God's oneness takes precedence over everything. The Shaykh of Kharaqan went so far as to remark, "On the Day of Judgment, when they question me, I will say: 'O God, do not ask Abu'l-Hasan about Abu'l-Hasan. Ask me about Your unity!'"

> Selfishness is faithlessness, and selflessness is faith;
> That is the gist and kernel of all I have to say.
> (*Kashf al-haqa'iq*)

DROP TWO

*I have not created
jinn and mankind
except to worship Me*

Prayer

ON THE NIGHT of the Messenger's Night Journey and Ascension, in a dazzling audience in the highest heaven at the station of *two-bows'-length*, God enjoined the Messenger and his community to offer up fifty prayers daily. As the Messenger descended, he met the Speaker. Hearing of the fifty prayers, the Speaker said, "Prayer is a weighty matter and your people are weak, so go back to your Lord and ask him to reduce the number for you and your community." The Messenger accordingly returned to God, and God reduced the number by ten. But the Speaker was still uneasy, so the Messenger requested another reduction. This went on until the number was whittled down to five. The Speaker suggested additional pleading, but the Messenger was unwilling to press the point any further. Concerning the five, the Messenger told his people, "He of you who performs them in faith and trust will have the reward of fifty prayers."

Each of the five prayers of the day is linked to a hallowed event in the lives of the prophets. Adam the Pure prayed the dawn prayer at the end of his first night on earth. Abraham the Friend prayed the midday prayer when he was commanded to render a sacrifice. Jonah prayed the afternoon prayer while in the belly of the whale. Jesus the Spirit prayed the evening prayer when he proclaimed the unity of God. Moses the Speaker prayed the night prayer on a storm-swept night in the desert while his wife suffered the pangs of childbirth and wolves attacked his flocks.

What does it mean to perform a prayer "in faith and trust"? The Messenger said, "There is no prayer without presence of the heart." A prayer is clear and true when the heart is unswayed by anything other than God.

> *Be you watchful over the prayers* (2:238)

> When I am with You, my every act is a prayer;
> But if I pray without You, my prayer's insincere.
> (*Kashkul-i Kalimi*)

A fool once took part in the congregational prayer on Friday. As the imam recited "Alhamdu li'Llah," the fool began mooing like a cow. When the prayer was finished someone demanded to know why he had done such a thing. The fool answered that he thought he was expected to follow the imam, and the imam was buying a cow. On inquiry, the imam admitted that the thought of buying a cow had crossed his mind at that moment.

> A prayer performed in an unfeeling manner
> Is a pile dust for the winds to scatter.
> (Sana'i)

Prayer is necessarily preceded by the act of ablution. The outer ablution consists in washing the hands, mouth, nose, and so forth, with water. The inner ablution consists in ridding the heart of pernicious thoughts. The inner ablution brings about a separation between the heart and the shadows of the world. Shibli remarks, "Ablution is separation, and prayer is union. Whoever does not separate does not unite!"

The worshiper must face the direction of prayer. The direction of prayer for Muslims is the direction of the Ka'ba. Previously, it was the direction of the Rock of Jerusalem. In the time before time, it was the direction of the Eternal—which is all directions, and no direction. Sharaf ad-Din Yahya, the Shaykh of Manayr, observes that the Rock and the Ka'ba have been pointed out to console the hearts of seekers in the house of sorrow that is the world. But he adds, "the direction of prayer for those who yearn for the Friend has become what it was in preeternity."

We will surely turn thee to a direction that shall
satisfy thee (2:144)

I see Your face and bow down then and there;
That in our creed is the meaning of prayer.
(Hasan)

A prayer begins with an intention. What is called for, in essence, is the intention to bear the burden of the Ancient Trust, which is heavier than anything on earth. The Lion of God, who was afraid of nothing, used to blanch and shake when the hour of prayer came. Someone asked him what was the matter. He answered, "There has come the time of the Covenant which God offered to *the heavens and the earth and the mountains, but they refused to carry it and were afraid of it* and I have carried it."

When worship commences, a dialogue ensues between creature and Creator. The Messenger said,

"Each one of you, when you pray, has an intimate talk with the Lord." The worshiper magnifies the Worshiped as the *Lord of all Being*, the *All-merciful*, the *All-compassionate*, and the *Master of the Day of Doom*. From the Worshiped come intimations of *succor* and guidance on *the straight path*.

The worshiper's imagination of God in prayer prepares the heart for the earth-shattering disclosure known as vision. The Messenger said, "Sincerity is to worship God as if you see Him, and if you do not see Him, know that He sees you."

> This is the shape of the secret, this, the veil of desire;
> When You appear before me, I know that this is
> prayer.
>
> (Raz)

The root of the word "prayer," *salat*, is S-L-W. It is a short step from S-L-W to W-S-L (as in *wasl*), which bespeaks conjunction and union. As sacred imagination paves the path to vision, vision opens the door to union. Sufi lore recalls the Messenger calling the prayer of essence, "Union with the *Lord of all Being*." In this prayer lies the fulfillment of the purpose of creation.

> *I have not created jinn and mankind except to*
> *worship Me* (51:56)

DROP THREE

*Those of you who
believe and expend
shall have a mighty wage*

Almsgiving

ABRAHAM THE FRIEND was known for his limitless hospitality. It was his custom to refrain from eating unless there was a guest to share his bread. Once it happened that three days passed without the arrival of a traveler. At last a visitor appeared, but when the Friend saw that the man was a fire worshiper he thought to turn him away. Suddenly the divine Voice rang in his ear, saying, "Will you not give a bit of cake to a person I have nourished for seventy years?"

> Why should the fact that he bows before fire
> Cause your hospitable hand to retire?
>
> (Sa'di)

Surely, Abraham was a nation obedient unto God, a Hanif, and no idolator. Those who followed the traditions of the Friend of God in Arabia were known as Hanifs. Every year, in the month of Ramadan, it was their practice to distribute alms to the needy.

When the Martyr of Baghdad visited the Holy Sepulcher in Jerusalem and the monks asked his religion, he answered, "I am a Hanif, the least significant Hanif of the Community of Muhammad."

> Become a Hanif of unrestricted vision;
> Enter, like a monk, the abbey of religion.
>
> (Shabistari)

The Messenger continued the traditions of the Friend. Ibn Ishaq tells of how, during Ramadan, the Messenger would "pray in seclusion and give food to the poor that came to him." The Hanifs called this method of spiritual retreat *tahannuth*. It was in the silence of tahannuth on Mount Hira', the "Mountain of Light," that revelation first came to the Messenger.

Prayer is the worship that is due from one's body. *Zakat*, or almsgiving, is the worship that is due from one's wealth. The Law obliges Muslims who enjoy sufficient means to give one-fortieth of what they own to the needy every year.

> *Those of you who believe and expend shall have a mighty wage* (57:7)

The Shaykh of Rum said, "Someone buries an insignificant seed in the ground and entrusts it to God. God Most High makes of that seed a tree that produces limitless fruit for the reason that it was entrusted to God."

> The hand that in almsgiving shows itself gracious,
> Will become, over there, a verdant oasis.
>
> (Rumi)

To test his knowledge of the Law, a doctor of law once asked Shibli how many coins should be expended as charity every year. Shibli inquired whether he wished to be told the practice of lawyers or the practice of God's poor. "Both," said the lawyer. Shibli answered, "According to the way of lawyers, after the elapse of a year, five out of every two hundred dirhams should be expended. According to the way of the poor, all two hundred dirhams should be expended immediately!"

The Messenger and his Companions lived lives of utmost simplicity. Abu Bakr the Sincere gave away all his possessions and 'Umar the Discriminator gave away half of what he owned. The Messenger asked each of them, "What remains for your family?" The Discriminator answered, "The equivalent of what I gave." The Sincere answered, "God and His Messenger!"

> Give whenever you can—do not be hesitant,
> For no generous act incurs a detriment.
>
> (Nakhshabi)

Giving is always for the good, especially when one gives others the things one enjoys oneself. It was the custom of 'Abd Allah ibn 'Umar to distribute sugar. He explained, "I have heard God say, *You will not attain the good until you expend of what you love,* and God knows I love sugar!"

Possessions have a way of possessing their possessor. To give is liberating. Nuri said, "The Sufi is one who possesses nothing and is possessed by nothing." An open hand opens the heart, and heaven's light shines through.

In reality, God is always the giver and the receiver. The Messenger said, "Alms fall into the hand of God, the Honored and Glorified, before they fall into the hand of the supplicant who receives them." One who knows this is delighted to distribute alms without any thought of return in this world or the next. Possessions are nothing; the Friend is everything.

Zu'n-Nun said, "Last night while I was in prostration, my eyes succumbed to sleep and I saw the Lord. He said, 'O Abu'l-Fayz, when I created humans they divided into ten parts. I offered them the material world, and nine of the ten parts turned their face toward it. One part remained, and they too divided into ten parts. I offered them paradise, and nine of the ten parts turned their faces toward it. One part remained, and they too divided into ten parts. I brought hell before them, and they were terrified and scattered in fear. Only one part remained, those who were neither seduced by the material world, nor drawn to paradise, nor afraid of hell. I said, 'My servants, you did not look at the material world, you were not drawn to paradise, and you were not afraid of hell. What are you looking for?' They all raised their heads and exclaimed, 'You know what we want!'"

DROP FOUR

Presecribed for you
is the Fast

Fasting

FASTING IS a tradition of the Prophets. The Speaker fasted for forty days on Mount Sinai. The Vicar's custom was to fast every other day. When Our Lady's son was due to be born, God instructed her, *say, "I have vowed to the All-merciful a fast, and today I will not speak to any man."* After his baptism at the hands of Saint John, the Spirit fasted for forty days in the wilderness. The Law of the Messenger prescribes fasting throughout the month of Ramadan.

> *O believers, prescribed for you is the Fast, even as*
> *it was prescribed for those that were before you*
>   (2:183)

Ramadan is the month of hot stones and cleansing rains. The fire of hunger cooks the bodies of believers, and the water of repentence washes their hearts.

> If He burns you, say, "Burn me!" If He soothes
>   you, say, "Soothe me!"
> Between fire and water is where a lover ought
>   to be.
>   (*Tafsir-i adabi va 'irfani*)

The Messenger said that fasting is "half of patience." Junayd accordingly calls fasting "half of the Path."

In addition to teaching patience, fasting teaches compassion. The one who fasts comes to learn what it means to be hungry. God made the Messenger an orphan and a stranger to acquaint him with the condition of the dispossessed.

As difficult as it may be to go without food and drink, there is pleasure in it when it is done for the sake of the One Who *feeds and is not fed*. When the belly is silent, the heart sings. The Messenger said, "The believer is a lute that makes music when it is empty."

> What sweetness hides in a belly void of food!
> A human being is very much like a lute:
> When the belly of a lute is all filled up,
> Its strings, high and low, go entirely mute.
> (Rumi)

The uniqueness of fasting as a practice of sacred devotion lies in its emptiness. Fasting is not so much an act as a renunciation of acts. As such, it cannot be compared with anything. Its incomparability serves as a sign of the incomparability of God: *Like Him there is naught*.

A sage said, "Fasting is absenting oneself from the vision of what is other than God for the sake of the vision of God Most High." To avert one's gaze from nonexistence is to turn toward Pure Being. Negation leads to affirmation; no god leads to *but God*.

> Rid the road of others if you wish to reach My place;
> Glance at no one else if you desire to see My Face.
> (Rumi)

The Messenger said, "For the one who fasts there are two joys: the joy of breaking the fast and the joy of meeting his Lord." God promises, *The fast is for Me and I am the reward which comes with it.*

The fast of the body is to abstain from food and drink. The fast of the spirit, on the contrary, is to partake of sustenance—but sustenance of a different kind. The Martyr of Hamadan, 'Ayn al-Quzat, says the food of the gnostic is "I pass the night with my Lord," and the drink of the gnostic is and *unto Moses God spoke directly.* God instructed the Sublime Defender, "O Sublime Defender, do not eat, do not drink, and do not sleep except with Me, with a present heart and a watchful spirit."

The Shaykh of Rum wrote these words in large letters on the wall of his madrasa:

> To fast from the food of the spirit is forbidden.
> But God knows best!

DROP FIVE

*Fulfil the Pilgrimage
and the
Visitation unto God*

Pilgrimage

WITH HIS SON Ishmael, Abraham the Friend built the granite cube known as the Ka'ba and consecrated it to the One Alone. In time, its caretakers lapsed into idolatry and the worship of the One was abandoned, except in the minds and hearts of a few staunch Hanifs. Such was the state of things in Mecca until the Messenger swept the idols from the House of the Lord and revived the faith of the Friend. A new era of pilgrimage was now proclaimed:

Fulfil the Pilgrimage and the Visitation unto God
(2:196)

The essence of a pilgrimage is its intention. Sufyan Sawri once heard a young man who longed to perform the Hajj give vent to an ardent sigh. Sufyan, who had completed the Hajj four times, offered to exchange the merit of his pilgrimages for the merit of the young man's sigh. The young man happily agreed. That night the divine Voice spoke to Sufyan in his dream, congratulating him on a profitable transaction.

Every Hajj you have made is now fully approved,
You are happy with God, and God is happy with
you.
('Attar)

Three pilgrimages, in fact, are known to the followers of the Messenger: that of the Law, that of the Path,
and that of the Truth. The pilgrimage of the Law is
a journey to the House of God *in the horizons*. The
Law ordains that the pilgrims must travel to Mecca and circumambulate the Ka'ba. The pilgrimage
of the Path is a journey *in themselves*. In this inner
journey, the pilgrims discover their own reality and
come to self-knowledge. The pilgrimage of the Truth
is to reach the Lord of the House, *If he is able to make
his way there*. This third pilgrimage was fulfilled by
Abraham the Friend when he lost himself in God and
exclaimed, *I have turned my face to Him who originated the heavens and the earth*.

The Shaykh of Bistam made all three journeys. He
explained, "On my first pilgrimage I saw nothing
but the House. The second time I saw the House and
the Lord of the House. The third time I saw only the
Lord, and did not see the House at all."

> The world is a form and its meaning is He;
> Look to the meaning and He's all that you'll see.
> (*Javahir al-'ushshaq*)

In the pilgrimage of the Truth, the one who is absent from God at Mecca may as well be at home, while
one who is present to God at home stands before the
inner reality of the Ka'ba. The Succor of the Poor observes, "Pilgrims circumambulate the Ka'ba with
their bodies, but gnostics circumambulate the divine
Throne and the Veil of Majesty with their hearts, de-
sirous of a tryst with God."

I was in pain, not for the Ka'ba but for Your
Countenance;
I was inebrious, not with wine but with Your
Redolence.
(Tafsir-i adabi va 'irfani)

The Shaykha of Basra once set out for Mecca. Along the way, the Ka'ba came to meet her. The shaykha said, "I need the Lord of the House; what am I to do with the House? I need to be met by the One Who said, *Whoever approaches me by a hand's span, I approach by an arm's span.*"

It wasn't love of the House that made my heart spin,
It was love of the One Who resided therein.
(Maktubat-i sadi)

The truth is that every illuminated breast is a sacred enclosure. The Messenger said, "The human heart is the House of the All-Merciful."

God told the Sublime Defender, "I have not shown Myself in anything in the way that I have shown Myself in the human being."

In your selves; what, do you not see? (51:21)

Without us He cannot be seen;
Without Him we possess no being.
(Javahir al-'ushshaq)

But not every human being is a clear reflection of the Creator. It is in the complete human being that God's light shines brightly. Because of their completeness, the friends of God became living Ka'bas.

The Shaykh of Bistam asked a man on the road, "Where are you going?" He answered, "To the House of God Most High." The shaykh asked, "How many dirhams do you have?" The man said, "Seven." The shaykh said, "Give them to me and circle me three times and you've made your pilgrimage."

The Succor of the Poor said, "There was a time when I circumambulated the Kaʿba, but now the Kaʿba circumambulates me."

> Don't bemoan the difference in ways,
> the Guide of the Way is one.
> Mosque and temple—You are both,
> pagoda and Kaʿba are one.
>
> (*Wujud al-ʿashiqin*)

CONCLUSION

One whose footstep is as light as a bubble
Can walk on water without any trouble.

　　　　　　　　　　　　　　　　—Ghani

Wave, drop, or bubble—whatever it be,
To the mystic's eye it's all simply sea.

　　　　　　　　　　　　　　　—Jamman

THE POLESTARS of the People of the Way had room in their hearts for all people. The mourning that followed their departure from the world was always universal. Ma'ruf Karkhi showed unlimited goodwill toward all faiths. When he passed away, believers of all denominations came and claimed him as their own. When Kabir died, the Muslims wished to bury his body while the Hindus proposed to cremate it. Legend tells that the opening of his shroud revealed only flowers, leaving both parties bewildered.

When the Shaykh of Rum died, the Jews and Christians of Konya grieved as keenly as the Muslims:

> All the religious communities were present with their spiritual and temporal leaders, including the Christians, the Jews, the Greeks, the Arabs, the Turks, and others. In accordance with tradition, they all walked in procession holding up their sacred books. They recited verses from the Psalms, the Torah, and the Gospels, and ut-

tered cries of lamentation. . . . The leading monks and priests were summoned and asked, "What does this event have to do with you? This king of religion is our leader, guide, and chief." They answered, "We have come to understand the reality of Jesus, of Moses, and of all of the prophets by means of his clear explanations, and we have witnessed in him the manner of the perfect prophets about whom we read in our books. Inasmuch as you Muslims call Mawlana the Muhammad of the age, we regard him as the Moses of the age and the Jesus of the age. Just as you are his adorers and devotees, we too are his servants and disciples, indeed a thousand times more so." As the poet said: "Seventy-two religions heard their secret from me / My flute unites a crowd of creeds in one sweet melody."

Wherever you may be, God will bring you all together (2:148)

Among the Folk of the Way, to harp on distinctions is considered a gaucherie. Kabir said, "Do not ask the caste of the gnostic." 'Abbas ibn Yusuf Shakli remarked, "Whoever is occupied with God, do not inquire concerning his faith."

To be of service, freedom's sons and daughters
Flow with all people like water with water.
(Sana'i)

Feuds over religion are typically fuelled by fear, anger, and vanity: the traits of the benighted ego. When the ego is effaced these tendencies naturally fade away, making way for courage, benevolence, and humility.

> Contempt and esteem are alike to me;
> My religion is the sum of all creeds.
>
> (*Hasanat al-'arifin*)

Anyone who investigates the revealed religions with an open mind and a discerning heart is bound to discover the truth in all of them. Of course, there are notable differences between them. Each faith is distinguished by the personality of its messenger and the circumstances of its revelation. With the passing of time, faith traditions are also subject to the proliferation of distorted interpretations. Nonetheless, to seeing eyes it is plain to see that all of the world's great faiths harbor at their core the same message of love.

> *God will assuredly bring a people He loves, and*
> *who love Him*   (5:54)

> The real infidel to us is love's enemy;
> What kind of faith condemns love as a heresy?
>
> (Jamman)

The Shaykh of Rum says, "On the Day of Judgement prayers will be brought forward and placed on the scale; fasts and alms likewise. But when they bring out love it will not fit on the scale. So the essential thing is love."

> In love there is a prayer devoid of prostration;
> Twixt Jew, Christian and Muslim love brooks no
>   distinction.
>
> (*Maktubat-i sadi*)

Through whichever channel Providence pours it out to the thirsty, the divine love that flows through revelation is from first to last a single substance. All fields are *watered with one water*. In the absence of

255

this pristine water, the world is a barren wasteland. In its presence, the earth grows lush and green. Flowers bloom, fruits ripen, and birds sing.

But words can only say a little.

> As you are a gnostic I'll be concise:
> For a gnostic a mere dot should suffice.
> ('Andalib)

And God alone is eternal.

Acknowledgments

THE AUTHOR wishes to warmly thank Sandra Lillydahl, Cannon Labrie, Jennifer Wittman, Deepa Patel, Joseph Aubert, Muhammad Yamin Ajaz, Nasrollah Pourjavady, Nancy Barta-Norton, Richard Gale, Martin Röhrs, Mehmet and Zehra Kasim, Deborah Morin, and Fatima Besharat for their help and support. *Shukriya!*

Notes

Note: Full publication data for the sources can be found in the bibliography. Unless otherwise stated, all translations from the Arabic, Persian, and Urdu are by the author.

Introduction

xi   *The true religion*   Inayat Khan, *Complete Works: Sayings I*, 118.

Bring me a   Amir Hasan Sijzi, *Fava'id al-fu'ad*, 226.

Mawlana Jalal ad-Din   Jalal ad-Din Rumi, *Masnavi-yi ma'navi*, 285–86.

xii   *In the blessed*   Rumi, *Masnavi*, 372. Compare *Katha Upanishad* 4:14–5, trans. Patrick Olivelle, 242: "As the rain that falls on rugged terrain, runs hither and thither along the mountain slopes; So a man who regards the laws as distinct, runs hither and thither after those very laws. As pure water poured into pure water becomes the very same; So does the self of a discerning sage become, O Gautama."

We make no   Qur'an 3:84, *The Koran Interpreted*, trans. A. J. Arberry. All citations from the Qur'an are from this edition.

The Sufi's Religion   Muhammad Husayni Gisu Daraz, *Mi'raj al-'ashiqin*, 20.

The religion of   Rumi, *Masnavi*, 216.

Love's the sole   Qutb ad-Din Bakhtiyar Kaki (att.), *Divan*, 73.

Beware of limiting   Muhyi ad-Din Ibn 'Arabi, *Fusus al-hikam*, 113.

xiii   *Amazing! A garden*   Muhyi ad-Din Ibn 'Arabi, *Tarjuman al-ashwaq*, 43–44.

Mansur Hallaj, the   Husayn ibn Mansur al-Hallaj, *Diwan*, 126. Hallaj then recited: "When, searchingly, I contemplated the creeds; I found one root—with many branches indeed!"

Waves of many   Muhammad Makhdum Husayn, *Mizan at-tawhid*, 65.

xiv   *Abu Sa'id ibn*   Muhammad bin Munavvar, *Asrar at-tawhid*, vol. 1, 210.

If you too   'Ayn al-Quzat Hamadani, *Tamhidat*, 285.

Every road I   Kay Khusraw Isfandiyar (att.), *Dabistan-i mazahib*, 3.

Light upon light   Qur'an 24:36.

Wave One: Dreaming of India

3   *The spirit of*   Rumi, *Masnavi*, 590.

You who fault   Amir Khusraw, *Khamsa*, 60.

Be we Muslim   Baba Tahir, *Divan*, 48.

Legend relates that   'Ali ar-Rumi quoted by Azad Bilgrami in Carl W. Ernst, "India as a Sacred Islamic Land," 559.

Sufism was intellectually   Inayat Khan, *Social Gathekas*.

Some speculate that   R. C. Zaehner, *Hindu and Muslim Mysticism*, 93–109.

Afterward he visited   Louis Massignon, *The Passion of al-Hallaj*, trans. Herbert Mason, vol. 1, 103.

Treatises on Yoga   Scott Kugle and Carl W. Ernst,

ed., *Sufi Meditation and Contemplation,* 181–92.

4   *Khvaja Qutb ad-Din's* Amir Hasan Sijzi, *Fava'id al-fu'ad,* 54–55, 245.

Later writers credit "Risala-yi azkar-i Chishtiya" in *Majmu'a-yi yazda rasa'il,* 11–13; Muhammad Chishti, *Majalis-i Hasaniya,* 7; Kalim Allah Jahanabadi, *Kashkul-i Kalimi,* 65; Nizam ad-Din Awrangabadi, *Nizam al-qulub,* 32.

For every people K. A. Nizami, *The Life and Times of Shaikh Nizamuddin Auliya,* 125.

5   *In his memoirs* Jahangir, *Tuzuk-i Jahangiri,* trans. A. Rogers and H. Beveridge, 356.

A vision of *Jug bashast,* trans. Muhammad Dara Shikuh, 4.

6   *He translated the* Upanishad (*Sirr-i akbar*), trans. Muhammad Dara Shikuh, vol. 1, v.

Paradise is a Muhammad Dara Shikuh, *Divan,* 104.

You say of Ibid., 181.

7   *The wise speak* *Rig Veda* 1.164. 46 quoted in Wendy Doniger, *On Hinduism,* 10.

The reality of Mirza Mazhar Jan-i Janan, *Khutut,* 94–95.

8   *There is no* Muhammad Taqi Niyazi, *Raz-i muhabbat,* 4–5.

The science of Hasan Nizami, *Hindu mazhab ki ma'lumat,* 6.

Sanusis in far-off Carl W. Ernst, "Traces of Shattari Sufism and Yoga in North Africa."

9   *Whoever denies the* Personal conversation with the author, New Lebanon, NY, 2000.

Many Turks and   Rumi, *Masnavi*, 50.

Drop One: The Water of Life

13   *There was neither*   *Rig Veda*, trans. Wendy Doniger, 25.

God is said   Ibn 'Arabi, *Fusus al-hikam*, 77.

God was, and   Hadith.

Rain and clay   Mahmud Shabistari, *Gulshan-i raz*, 53.

14   *There was neither*   *Rig Veda*, trans. Doniger, 25.

I love not   Qur'an 6:76.

To the sage   *Yoga Vasishtha*, trans. Swami Venkatesananda, vol. 1, 91.

From beginning to   Mir Dard, *Divan*, 123.

That one breathed   *Rig Veda*, trans. Doniger, 25.

There was air   Hadith: "He was in *al-'ama* having no air above or beneath it."

Darkness was hidden   *Rig Veda*, trans. Doniger, 25.

Formless and bottomlessly   Akbar Husayni, *Tabsirat al-istilahat as-sufiya*, 140.

Know that death   Rumi, *Masnavi*, 439.

Shah Kalim Allah   Kalim Allah Jahanabadi, *Kashkul-i Kalimi*, 26.

15   *Desire came upon*   *Rig Veda*, trans. Doniger, 25.

I was a   Hadith Qudsi.

From root to trunk   lahut: the divine plane; jabarut: the spiritual plane; malakut: the mental plane; nasut: the physical plane.

Whence this creation   *Rig Veda*, trans. Doniger, 25.

Contemplate the divine   Hadith.

16   *The inability to*   Ibn 'Arabi, *Fusus al-hikam*, 62.

No one can   Abu'l-Majd Majdud Sana'i, *Hadiqat al-haqiqat*, 63.

By what means   'Ayn al-Quzat Hamadani, *Difa'iyat*, 51.

You know 'how"   Farid ad-Din 'Attar, *Tazkirat al-awliya'*, 95.

Whoso knows God   Hadith.

Bring me, Saqi   Fakhr ad-Din 'Iraqi, *Kulliyat*, 137.

Drop Two: The Great Soul

19   *Its founder Hiranyagarbha*   *Mahabharata*, trans. Pratapa Chandra Ray, vol. 7, 590.

From love the   Muhammad Dara Shikuh, *Majma' al-bahrayn*, 4.

The sun in   Akbar Hadi, *Sharh-i hal-i Mir Damad va Mir Findiriski ba-inzimam-i divan-i Mir Damad va qasida-yi Mir Findiriski*, 99.

The wine became   Rumi, *Masnavi*, 72.

20   *The first thing*   Hadith.

a radiant lamp   Qur'an 33:46.

I was a   Hadith.

The light in   Ahmad Jam, *Divan*, 16.

Hiranyagarbha, says Shankaracharya   *Eight Upanishads*, trans. Swami Gambhirananda, vol. 2, 475.

What are the   Fakhr ad-Din 'Iraqi, *Kulliyat*, 375.

The hearts of   Hadith.

This age-old 'Abd al-Qadir Bidil, *Shu'la-avaz*, 314.

21 *The human form* Kalim Allah Jahanabadi, *Sawa' as-sabil*, 144.

From this very *Taittiriya Upanishad* 2:1 in *Upanishads*, trans. Olivelle, 185.

And from the Mu'in ad-Din Chishti (att.), *Risala*, fol. 5b.

The human is Hadith Qudsi.

But for you Ibid.

God bless and Nur al-Hasan Sahasvani, *Naghmat-i sama'*, 18.

Drop Three: Maya

25 *With maya He* Shvetashvatara Upanishad 4:9–10, *Upanishads*, trans. Juan Mascaro, 92.

Gaudapadacharya, in his *Mandukya Karika* 4:47–50 quoted in *Sixty Upanishads of the Veda*, 631–32.

A subtle ruse Mahmud Shabistari, *Gulshan-i raz*, 74.

26 *The movement that* Ibn 'Arabi, *Fusus al-hikam*, 203.

Hence Dara Shikuh Dara Shikuh, *Majma' al-bahrayn*, 4.

Who is Adam? Muhammad Husayni Gisu Daraz, *Wujud al-'ashiqin*, 4.

Though unborn, It Yajur Veda 31:19 quoted in *Sudhakshina Rangaswami, The Roots of Vedanta*, p. 238.

This "I" and: Rumi, *Masnavi*, 71.

no mere pastime Qur'an 21:16.

God has set Qur'an 9:93.

Composed of nature's The Bhagavad-Gita, trans. Barbara Stoler Miller, 73.

27 *It is sprung* 14 Anugita 47:12, *Mahabharata*, trans. Ray, vol. 9, 120 (modified). Cf. F. D. K. Bosch, *The Golden Germ*, 67.

This world is Rumi, *Masnavi*, 340.

I looked and Abu Nasr as-Sarraj, *Kitab al-luma'*, 464.

Drop Four: Food

31 *Respect bread, enjoined* Muhammad al-Ghazali, *Ihya' 'ulum ad-din*, vol. 2, 6.

One should not Taittiriya Upanishad 3:7, *Upanishads*, trans. Olivelle, 191.

If 'isha and Muhammad al-Ghazali, *Ihya' 'ulum ad-din*, vol. 2, 6.

A morsel is Rumi, *Masnavi*, 66.

I am food Taittiriya Upanishad 3:10, *Upanishads*, trans. Olivelle, 193.

The refreshment of 'Abd al-Karim al-Qushayri, *ar-Risala*, 72.

The body of Maitri Upanishad 6:13, *Hindu Scriptures*, trans. R. C. Zaehner, 230.

32 *Rapture comes when* J. L. Masson and M. V. Patwardhan, *Aesthetic Rapture*, vol. 1, 23–35.

The soul is Ibid., 18.

As the body's 'Ali Hujviri, *Kashf al-mahjub*, 507.

Here is a 'Attar, *Tazkirat al-awliya'*, 207.

Let me see   Fakhr ad-Din ʿIraqi, *Kulliyat*, 396.

The alchemy that   ʿAziz ad-Din Nasafi, *Kitab al-insan al-kamil*, 91.

Eat all manner   Qurʾan 16:69.

Wherein is healing   Ibid., 16:70.

Whoever, like the   Rumi, *Masnavi*, 900.

33   *Just as the*   Chandogya Upanishad 6:9.

This self is   Brhadaranyaka Upanishad, *Upanishads*, trans. Olivelle, 32.

Because He craved   Maitri Upanishad 6:12, *Hindu Scriptures*, trans. Zaehner, 230.

If for Himself   Ibn ʿArabi, *Fusus al-hikam*, 187. Ibn ʿArabi refers to food here in the sense of nourishment (*ghidha*ʾ) rather than physical food (*taʿam*). The Qurʾan states that God has no need of the latter (6:14 and 51:57).

You are His   Ibn ʿArabi, *Fusus al-hikam*, 83.

Where is His   Ibid., 83.

34   *When one experiences*   Vijnana Bhairava, trans. Jaideva Singh, 68.

I pass the   Hadith.

Bread is God's   Farid ad-Din ʿAttar, *Musibatnama*, 359.

Drop Five: The Chariot

37   *He who has*   Amir Hasan Sijzi, *Favaʾid al-fuʾad*, 175.

Dress yourself in   Muhammad Ziyaʾ al-Hasan Jili Kalimi, *Kalam-i Ziyaʾ*, 132.

Tell me what   Katha Upanishad 2:14, *Upanishads*, trans. Olivelle, 237.

If you seek   Farid ad-Din 'Attar, *Divan*, 190.

38   *The wise one*   *Katha Upanishad* 2:18, *Upanishads*, trans. Olivelle, 237.

Be not without   Ahmad Ghazali, *Majmu'a-yi asar-i Farsi*, 322.

When someone told   Muhammad bin Munavvar, *Asrar at-tawhid*, vol. 1, 203.

Never is there   Muhammad Nasir 'Andalib, *Nala-yi 'Andalib*, 643.

The self that   *Katha Upanishad*, 3:3–4.

With love our   Ahmad Ghazali, *Majmu'a-yi asar-i Farsi*, 115.

39   *The rider of*   Muhammad Husayni Gisu Daraz, *Javahir al-'ushshaq*, 17.

Unto God is   Qur'an 3:28.

Higher than the   *Katha Upanishad* 3:10–11, *Upanishads*, trans. Olivelle, 239.

The journey to   Kalim Allah Jahanabad, *Kashkul-i Kalimi*, 3.

Razor's edge   *Katha Upanishad* 3:14, *Upanishads*, trans. Olivelle, 240.

The way is   Ziya' al-Hasan Jili Kalimi, *Kalam-i Ziya'*, 142.

40   *Living, honey-eating*   *Katha Upanishad* 4:5, *Upanishads*, trans. Olivelle, 241.

Nearer . . . than the   Qur'an 50:16.

From death to   *Katha Upanishad* 4:11, *Upanishads*, trans. Olivelle, 242.

Lord of what   Ibid., 4:13, 242.

Changeless among the   Ibid., 5:13, 244.

Lies awake within   Ibid., 5:8, 243.

slumber seizes Him   Qur'an 2:255.

So indeed is   Katha Upanishad 6:1, *Upanishads*, trans. Olivelle, 245.

The thunder proclaims   Qur'an 13:13.

As in a   Katha Upanishad 6:5, *Katha Upanishad*, trans. Joseph Rawson, 187.

The faithful is   Hadith.

Nonbeing is the   Mahmud Shabistari, *Gulshan-i raz*, 16.

Does not grieve   Katha Upanishad 6:6, *Upanishads*, trans. Olivelle, 245.

41   *Cessation of thought*   Patanjali, *Yoga Sutra*, trans. Barbara Stoler Miller, 29.

He attains the   Qur'an 6:103.

Neither My heaven   Hadith Qudsi.

No one can see: Katha Upanishad 6:9, *Upanishads*, trans. Olivelle, 245.

Wave Two: Even Unto China

45   *Budhasaf and the*   Shahab ad-Din Yahya Suhravardi, *Majmu'a-yi musannafat-i Shaykh-i Ishraq*, vol. 2, 217.

Shakyamuni is to   Iqbalshah Sijistani, *Chihil majlis*, 84.

46   *Its foremost monastery*   Christopher Beckwith, in *Warriors of the Cloisters*, describes how the Sarvastivadin scholastic method taught at Naw Bahar and the other *viharas* provided the

foundation for the Islamic madrasa, which in turn informed the creation of the medieval Christian college. In *Buddhism in Iran* (102–9), Mostafa Vaziri argues that the architecture of Naw Bahar and other Buddhist monuments likewise proved influential, finding reflection in Sufi and Shi'i shrines in Iran that resemble stupas.

When the Barmakids   See Johan Elverskog, *Buddhism and Islam on the Silk Road*, and Kevin van Bladel, "The Bactrian Background of the Barmakids."

Iran must have   Alessandro Bausani, "Religion under the Mongols," 541.

47   *He was a:*   Iqbalshah Sijistani, *Chihil majlis*, 82–83.

49   *You ate their*   'Attar, *Tazkirat al-awliya'*, 93–94.

In the following   Khache Phalu, *Advice on the Art of Living.*

During the same   See Sachiko Murata, *Chinese Gleams of Sufi Light,* and David Lee, *Contextualization of Sufi Spirituality in Seventeenth- and Eighteenth-Century China.*

50   *Zen is not*   Nyogen Senzaki, *Sufism and Zen,* 2–4, 6–7.

51   The Arabic word *murshid* means "spiritual guide."

Drop One: Awakening

55   *In that meadow*   Rumi, *Masnavi*, 719.

Queen Maya could   Ashva-ghosha, *Life of the Buddha*, 43.

56   *If you say*   Rumi, *Masnavi*, 56.

Surely death, from   Qur'an 62:8.

The wheel of   Husayn Va'iz Kashifi, *Anvar-i suhayli*, 35.

Death suffices as   Muhammad al-Ghazali, *Ihya' 'ulum ad-din*, vol. 5, 194.

This death has   Ibid., 195.

Choose another friend   Farid ad-Din 'Attar, *Mantiq at-tayr*, 172.

The demise of   Ziya' ad-Din Nakhshabi, *Silk as-suluk*, 104.

The farthest shore   Ashva-ghosha, *The Life of the Buddha*, 159.

57   *The ascetic is*   'Attar, *Divan*, 391.

Surely my Lord   Qur'an 11:56.

I'll not break   Ashva-ghosha, *The Life of the Buddha*, 371.

Sufism is sitting   'Attar, *Tazkirat al-awliya'*, 715–16.

The devil and   Rumi, *Masnavi*, 445.

God asked the   Jalal ad-Din Rumi, *Fihi ma fih*, 128.

58   *There is nothing*   Muhammad bin Munavvar, *Asrar at-tawhid*, vol. 1, 48.

Each fool that   Husayn Va'iz Kashifi, *Anvar-i suhayli*, 210.

Being desire from   Mir Taqi Mir, *Kulliyat*, 157.

59   *Volitional formations give*   Samyutta Nikaya quoted in Bhikkhu Bodhi, ed., *In the Buddha's Words*, 353.

When there was   Asad Allah Khan Ghalib, *Divan* (Urdu), 33.

You saw the Sadiq Hidayat, *Taranaha-yi Khayyam*, 101.

60 *Difficult is the* *The Dhammapada*, trans. John Ross Carter and Mahinda Palihawadana, 34 (modified).

It's difficult for Asad Allah Khan Ghalib, *Divan* (Urdu), 22.

Drop Two: Steps to Freedom

63 *By oneself is* *The Dhammapada*, trans. Carter and Palihawadana, 31.

Shall the recompense Qur'an 55:60.

Certainly they are Hadith.

By his own Ziya' ad-Din Nakhshabi, *Silk as-suluk*, 42.

64 *While sinners repent* Muslih Sa'di, *Kulliyat*, 63.

The Sufi is 'Attar, *Tazkirat al-awliya'*, 650.

There is no Hadith.

Everyone pleads his Muhammad Nasir 'Andalib, *Nala-yi 'Andalib*, 396.

O Lord, if 'Attar, *Tazkirat al-awliya'*, 106.

I did not Amir Hasan Sijzi, *Fava'id al-fu'ad*, 185–86.

Without the Beloved's Ziya' ad-Din Nakhshabi, *Silk as-suluk*, 140.

65 *Who, having abandoned* *The Dhammapada*, trans. Carter and Palihawadana, 70 (modified).

It is Layla Ahmad Shah Chishti Mawdudi, *Nava-yi Chishtiyan*, 38.

O monks, there Udana quoted in Walpola Rahula, *What the Buddha Taught*, 37 (modified).

What makes a   Muhammad Nasir 'Andalib,
Nala-yi 'Andalib, 554.

God placed all   'Abd al-Karim al-Qushayri,
ar-Risala, 96.

66   *You will not*   Qur'an 3:92 (modified).

For a person   'Aziz ad-Din Nasafi, *Kitab al-
insan al-kamil*, 331.

They asked the   Ibid., 231.

My mercy embraces   Qur'an 7:156.

Riverine generosity, sunny   Muhammad
Mubarak Kirmani, *Siyar al-awliya'*, 46.

Not by enmity   The Dhammapada, trans. Carter
and Palihawadana, 5.

As for he   Amir Hasan Sijzi, *Fava'id al-fu'ad*, 86.

All those who   Shantideva, The Way of the
Bodhisattva, trans. Padmakara Translation
Group, 49.

67   *The way of*   Amir Hasan Sijzi, *Fava'id al-fu'ad*, 87.

The chevalier has   'Abd al-Karim al-Qushayri,
ar-Risala, 177.

In the battle   The Dhammapada, trans. Carter
and Palihawadana, 20.

I have made   Muhammad Riza Shafi'i Kadkani,
Nivishta bar darya, 173.

Easily seen is   The Dhammapada, trans. Carter
and Palihawadana, 45.

Heedless of myself   Bahadur Shah Zafar, *Divan*, 32.

68   *Two intelligent people*   Muslih Sa'di, *Kulliyat*, 111.

By harmlessness toward   *The Dhammapada*,
trans. Carter and Palihawadana, 47.

Whoever passes a   Muhammad Riza Shafi'i
Kadkani, *Nivishta bar darya*, 251.

Righteous wealth righteously   Bhikkhu Bodhi,
ed., *In the Buddha's Words*, 126.

We appointed day   Qur'an 78:11.

Those who struggle   Ibid, 29:69.

One who does   'Abd al-Karim al-Qushayri,
ar-Risala, 81.

On the path   Abu'l-Majd Majdud Sana'i,
Hadiqat al-haqiqat, 141.

69   *The People of*   'Abd al-Karim al-Qushayri,
ar-Risala, 73.

Sufism is the   'Attar, *Tazkirat al-awliya'*, 715.

Every breath ofv   'Attar, *Mantiq at-tayr*, 172.

Over a single   Muhammad bin Munavvar,
Asrar at-tawhid, vol. 1, 247.

When he stands   Muhyi ad-Din Ibn 'Arabi,
*Tanbihat 'ala 'uluw al-haqiqat al-Muhammadiya
wa yalihi Ruh al-quds fi muhasabat an-nafs*, 131.

When thou threwest   Qur'an 8:17.

As a servant   'Abd ar-Rahman as-Sulami,
Tabaqat as-sufiya, 311.

70   *The elements are*   Rumi, *Masnavi*, 458.

When you remember   Muhammad al-Ghazali,
Ihya' 'ulum ad-din, vol. 5, 196.

When you give   Muhammad Husayni Gisu Daraz,
Wujud al-'ashiqin, 8.

Here the seeker   summary of the *Satipatthana Sutta* in Bhikkhu Bodhi, *The Noble Eightfold Path*, 90–91.

71   *Watching one's inner*   Muhammad al-Ghazali, *Ihya' 'ulum ad-din*, vol. 5, 129.

Though God's face   Muhammad Riza Shafi'i Kadkani, *Sha'ir-i ayinaha*, 306.

Unification is the   'Ali Hujviri, *Kashf al-mahjub*, 360.

An hour in   Muhammad Riza Shafi'i Kadkani, *Nivishta bar darya*, 251.

Enjoy this moment   Sadiq Hidayat, *Taranaha-yi Khayyam*, 103.

The one the   Mas'ud Bakk, *Divan*, 24.

Monarch on the   Kalim Allah Jahanabadi, *Kashkul-i Kalimi*, 46.

72   *The world exists*   Muhammad Riza Shafi'i Kadkani, *Sha'ir-i ayina-ha*, 307.

Beyond the sphere   Sangiti Sutta 3:264, *The Long Discourses of the Buddha*, trans. Maurice Walshe, 506.

Becoming of self   'Attar, *Mantiq at-tayr*, 248.

The conditioned becomes   Nur ad-Din 'Abd ar-Rahman Jami, *Lava'ih*, 58. Cf. Kalim Allah Jahanabadi, *Kashkul-i Kalimi*, 3.

Your loveliness exceeds   Ahmad Ghazali, *Majmu'a-yi asar-i Farsi*, 121.

Drop Three: Paradox

75   *Someone who has*   *Buddhist Wisdom*, trans. Edward Conze, 15–16.

In the path   'Abd al-Qadir Bidil, *Divan*, 78.

A voice once Habib 'Ali Shah, *Divan-i Habib*, 134–35.

76 *A Sufi is* Muhammad bin Munavvar, *Asrar at-tawhid*, vol. 1, 261. Cf. 'Attar, *Tazkirat al-awliya'*, 715.

And yet, although Buddhist Wisdom, trans. Conze, 16.

This talk of Nur ad-Din 'Abd ar-Rahman Jami, *Lava'ih*, 76.

A bodhisattva who Buddhist Wisdom, trans. Conze, 18.

Sincerity is lifting Abu Bakr al-Kalabadhi, *at-Ta'arruf li-madhhab ahl at-tasawwuf*, 117.

Wherever there is Buddhist Wisdom, trans. Conze, 20.

What of Adam Nur al-Hasan Sahasvani, *Naghmat-i sama'*, 221.

77 *And these Bodhisattvas* Buddhist Wisdom, trans. Conze, 23.

We make no Qur'an 3:84.

This dharma which Buddhist Wisdom, trans. Conze, 30.

It's your ego Abu'l-Majd Majdud Sana'i, *Hadiqat al-haqiqat*, 112.

Sufism is polytheism 'Ali Hujviri, *Kashf al-mahjub*, 43. Cf. Attar, *Tazkirat al-awliya'*, 715.

If . . . it would Buddhist Wisdom, trans. Conze, 40.

78 *If someone says* Muhammad bin Munavvar, *Asrar at-tawhid*, vol. 1, 252. Cf. 'Attar, *Tazkirat al-awliya'*, 276.

The bodhisattva, the Buddhist Wisdom, trans. Conze, 45.

If the eyes Inayat Khan, *Supplementary Papers* (Metaphysics 1, The Journey to the Goal).

They do not Entry into the Realm of Reality, trans. Thomas Cleary, 333.

Naught holds them Qur'an 16:79.

I am the Muhammad Munir ad-Din Mahmudi, *Shajarat al-Mahmud*, 157.

When the king Buddhist Wisdom, trans. Conze, 52.

At the battle Ahmad Maybudi, *Tafsir-i adabi va 'irfani-yi Qur'an-i majid*, vol. 1, 25.

79 *Said the Lion* Abu'l-Majd Majdud Sana'i, *Hadiqat al-haqiqat va shari'at at-tariqat*, 140.

"Tathagata" is called Buddhist Wisdom, trans. Conze, 64.

What is Sufism? 'Attar, *Tazkirat al-awliya'*, 717.

Nothing could be Sadiq Hidayat, *Taranaha-yi Khayyam*, 74.

As stars, a Buddhist Wisdom, trans. Conze, 69.

Drop Four: Form and Emptiness

83 *Moving in the* Buddhist Wisdom, trans. Conze, 82.

Why is the 'Attar, *Mantiq at-tayr*, 144.

Here, O Shariputra Buddhist Wisdom, trans. Conze, 86.

84 *All things within* 'Abd al-Qadir Bidil, *Shu'la-avaz*, 679.

Who is here Ibn 'Arabi, *Fusus al-hikam*, 122.

The Unconditioned does Nur ad-Din 'Abd
ar-Rahman Jami, *Lava'ih*, 79.

In separation I Ahmad Ghazali, *Majmu'a-yi
asar-i Farsi*, 189.

are in uncertainty Qur'an 50:15.

85 *Creation is always* Mahmud Shabistari, *Gulshan-i
raz*, 70.

O God, this Muhammad al-Ghazali, *Ihya'
'ulum ad-din*, vol. 1, 417.

When the heaps Walpola Rahula, *What the
Buddha Taught*, 33.

The world is Rumi, *Masnavi*, 47.

Just as the 'Ayn al-Quzat Hamadani, *Zubdat
al-haqa'iq*, 60.

In emptiness . . . there Buddhist Wisdom, trans.
Conze, 97.

Ahmad Chishti and Nur ad-Din 'Abd ar-Rahman
Jami, *Nafahat al-'uns*, 30.

86 *Gone, gone, gone* Buddhist Wisdom, trans.
Conze, 113.

Wave Three: Magian Wine

89 *The faith of* Abu'l-Majd Majdud Sana'i, *Divan*, 26.

I will gird 'Umar Khayyam, *Les Quatrains de
Khèyam*, trans. Nicolas, 123 (Persian text).

Stain your prayer Shams ad-Din Muhammad
Hafiz, *Divan*, 71.

It is said Bahram bin Farhad, *Sharistan-i chahar
chaman*, 193–94.

And messengers we Qur'an 4:164.

We have sent   Ibid 14:4.

According to the   Shahab ad-Din Yahya
Suhravardi, *Majma'-yi mussanafat-i Shaykh-i
Ishraq*, vol. 1, 502–3; vol. 2, 157.

90   *Suhravardi explains that*   Ibid., vol. 2, 10–11.

Suhravardi's cosmology envisions   For a succinct
summary of Suhravardi's angelology, see Ian
Richard Netton, *Allah Transcendent*, 260–68.

91   *At the court*   Abu'l-Fazl 'Allami draws on
Suhravardi's theory of the philosopher-king in
A'in-i Akbari, trans. A. Blochmann, 50.

Every flame is   Abu'l-Fazl 'Allami, *A'in-i Akbari*,
trans. Blochmann, 50.

Akbar's interest in: Kay Khusraw Isfandiyar,
Dabistan-i mazahib, vol. 1, 300–301.

92   *The eminent sages*   Ibid., 31.

95   *Science finds the*   Khuda-jui, *Jam-i Kay Khusraw*, 41.

The Zoroastrian heritage   Jacques Dushesne-
Guillemin, *Symbols and Values in Zoroastrianism*, 162.

It may be   Azar Kayvan's circle treated the
designations *ishraqi* (Illuminationist) and *sufi*
as synonymous. Bahram ibn Farhad, *Sharistan-i
chahar chaman*, 229.

Drop One: The Ahunvar

99   *This omniscience and*   Zand-Akasih: Iranian or
Greater Bundahishn, trans. Behramgore
Tehmuras Anklesaria, 5 (1:1–2).

Everything is His   Muhammad al-Ghazali, *Mishkat
al-anwar*, 60.

Ahriman never existed   Aturpat-i Emetan,
The Wisdom of the Sasanian Sages (Denkart
VI), trans. Shaul Shaked, 109.

100   *The will of*   *Sacred Books of the East: The Zend
Avesta*, Part I, trans. James Darmesteter, 210.

Of all things   *Sacred Books of the East: Pahlavi
Texts*, Part I, trans. E. W. West, 157.

Matter is animated   Sharaf ad-Din Manayri,
Maktubat-i sadi, 166.

The law is   Mas'ud Bakk, *Mir'at al-'arifin*, 3.

The gifts of   *Sacred Books of the East: The
Zend Avesta*, Part I, trans. Darmesteter, 210.

101   *The first perfection*   *Sacred Books of the East:
Pahlavi Texts*, Part V, trans. E. W. West, 157
(modified).

Every species on   Shahab ad-Din Yahya
Suhravardi, *Majmu'a-yi musannafat-i Shaykh-
Ishraq*, vol. 2, 128; Bahram bin Farhad,
Sharistan-i chahar chaman, 189.

The Good Mind   Shahab ad-Din Yahya
Suhravardi, *Majmu'a-yi musannafat-i Shaykh-i
Ishraq*, vol. 2, 200–201.

Whoever shall do   *Sacred Books of the East:
Pahlavi Texts*, Part V, trans. West, 158.

I have never   Aturpat-i Emetan, *The Wisdom
of the Sasanian Sages*, trans. Shaked, 183.

102   *Son, if you'd*   Rumi, *Masnavi*, 33.

O Lord, have   Muslih Sa'di, *Kulliyat*, 175.

Heaven is love's   Muhsin Fayz Kashani, *Divan-i
kamil*, 402.

surely God forgives   Qur'an 39:53.

When mercy enfolds   Muhyi ad-Din Ibn 'Arabi, *Futuhat al-makkiya*, vol. 2, 207.

In neither world   Zartusht Bahram bin Pazhdu, *Zaratushtnama*, 31.

Pass over, true   Hadith.

Whoever would be   Muhammad Mubarak Kirmani, *Siyar al-awliya'*, 45.

103   *He who relieves*   *Sacred Books of the East: The Zend Avesta*, Part I, trans. Darmesteter, 210.

To speak candidly   Muslih Sa'di, *Kulliyat*, 233.

The sovereignty of   *Sacred Books of the East: Pahlavi Texts*, Part V, trans. West, 157–58 (modified).

The food of   Gisu Daraz, *Javahir al-'ushshaq*, 13.

Drop Two: Angels and Adversaries

107   *In each sphere*   Kay Khusraw Isfandiyar (att.), *Dabistan-i mazahib*, vol. 1, 32.

In the heavens   Muhammad Nasir 'Andalib, *Nala-yi 'Andalib*, 448.

108   *The devil flows*   Hadith.

A thing that   Aturpat-i Emetan, *The Wisdom of the Sasanian Sages*, trans. Shaked, 173.

When Ahriman is   Ibid., 103.

The dispelling of   Ibid., 55.

My companions are   Rumi, *Masnavi*, 141.

When Akoman, the   Aturpat-i Emetan, *The Wisdom of the Sasanian Sages*, trans. Shaked, 75.

With clear wine   Bu 'Ali Shah Qalandar, *Divan*, 166.

109 *The satisfaction of*   Aturpat-i Emetan, *The Wisdom of the Sasanian Sages*, trans. Shaked, 75 (modified).

It is necessary to   Ibid., 75.

Send out, Lord   Imdad Allah Muhajir Makki, *Kulliyat-i Imdadiya*, 383.

By means of   Aturpat-i Emetan, *The Wisdom of the Sasanian Sages*, trans. Shaked, 95.

The love of   Ibid., 215.

It's no labor   Muhammad Dara Shikuh, *Risala-yi Haqq-numa*, 6.

When divine light   Ahmad Maybudi, *Tafsir-i adabi va 'irfani-yi Qur'an-i majid*, vol. 2, 127.

He brings them   Qur'an 2:257.

Drop Three: Fire

113 *The source of*   Zand-Akasih, trans. Anklesaria, 39.

The magi enumerate   Ibid., 157–58.

If it's not   Asad Allah Khan Ghalib, *Divan* (Urdu), 75.

The fires that   Khuda-jui bin Namdar, *Jam-i Kay Khusraw*, 12.

114 *When the traveler*   Ibid.

When a man   Aturpat-i Emetan, *The Wisdom of the Sasanian Sages*, trans. Shaked, 135.

If your spirit   Farid ad-Din 'Attar, *Asrarnama*, 117.

Whoever is in   Husayn Va'iz Kashifi, *Rashahat*, 123.

If there is   Muhammad al-Baqi, *'Irfaniyat-i Baqi*, 126.

Sometimes the flashes   Shahab ad-Din Yahya
Suhravardi, *Majmu'a-yi musannafat-i Shaykh-i
Ishraq*, vol. 3, 320–21.

115   *I saw numerous*   Khuda-jui bin Namdar, *Jam-i
Kay Khusraw*, 10.

It is He   Qur'an 13:12.

The Heavy Clouds   Qur'an 2:248, 9:40, 9:26,
48:3, 48:18, and 48:26.

Glorious is your   *The Desatir*, vol. 1, 166
(Asmani/Persian text).

A wave of   Jamal ad-Din Jamman, *Muntakhba-yi
divan*, 2.

Its recipient becomes   Shahab ad-Din Yahya
Suhravardi, *Majmu'a-yi musannafat-i Shaykh-i
Ishraq*, vol. 1, 504.

If God loves   Hadith.

116   *The Zend Avesta*   *Sacred Books of the East: The
Zend-Avesta*, Part II, trans. James Darmesteter,
286–309.

The days of   Abu'l-Qasim Firdawsi, *Shahnama*,
vol. 1, 45.

In a body   'Abd ar-Razzaq Kashani, *Istilahat
as-sufiya*, 20.

The power of   Khuda-jui bin Namdar, *Jam-i
Kay Khusraw*, 7.

I cast off   Ibid., 44.

117   *Love is fire*   Gisu Daraz, *Wujud al-'ashiqin*, 2.

Whoosh! and my   Qutb ad-Din Bakhtiyar Kaki
(att.), *Divan*, 72.

If a burning   Mu'in ad-Din Chishti (att.),
Divan-i Gharib Navaz, 23.

Then a marvel   Najm ad-Din Kubra, *Kitab
fawa'ih al-jamal wa fawatih al-jalal*, 39.

The phenomenal   Akbar Husayni, *Tabsirat
al-istilihat as-sufiya*, 24.

It is He   Ibn 'Arabi, *Al-futuhat al-makkiya*,
vol. 2, 326.

The forgetting of   Shahab ad-Din Yahya
Suhravardi, *Majmu'a-yi musannafat-i Shaykh-i
Ishraq*, vol. 3, 320–21.

As our hearts   'Attar, *Divan*, 489.

118   *O fire of*   Almut Hintze, *A Zoroastrian Liturgy*, 33.

Drop Four: the Living Earth

121   *May we be*   Yasna 30:9, *The Hymns of
Zoroaster*, trans. M.L. West, 55.

encircling about the   Qur'an 39:75.

After the audience   *Sacred Books of the East:
Pahlavi Texts*, Part V, trans. West, 161.

Whoever is kind   Hadith.

He will certainly   Zartusht Bahram bin Pazhdu,
Zaratushtnama, 32.

122   *That light is*   Ibid., 33.

I hereby proclaim   Ibid., 35.

You must convey   Ibid., 36.

123   *To man and beast*   Ibid.

Animals should be Sacred Books of the East: *Pahlavi Texts*, Part V, trans. West, 295.

Mubad Hushyar Kay Khusraw Isfandiyar, *Dabistan-i mazahib*, vol. 1, 25.

124 *nothing is, that* Qur'an 17:44.

"Be happy,"' said Farid ad-Din 'Attar, *Ilahinama*, 149.

White jasmine belongs Sacred Books of the East: *Pahlavi Texts*, Part I, trans. West, 104.

In tulip and rose Asad Allah Khan Ghalib, *Divan* (Urdu), 89.

Mountains and rivers Sacred Books of the East: *Pahlavi Texts*, Part III, L. H. Mills, 98.

To fire, air The Desatir, vol. 1, 11 (Asmani/ Persian text).

To please their Rumi, *Masnavi*, 36.

Do not curse Hadith.

Whoever cherishes the Zartusht Bahram bin Pazhdu, *Zaratushtnama*, 27.

Wave Four: The Staff of Moses

129 *I have heard* Shahab ad-Din Yahya Suhravardi, *Majmu'a-yi musannafat-i Shaykh-i Ishraq*, vol. 3, 332.

As for the Abu'l-Majd Majdud Sana'i, *Divan*, 105.

Because of you Muhammad bin Munavvar, *Asrar at-tawhid*, vol. 1, 331.

Shaykh Sharaf ad-Din Sharaf ad-Din Yahya Manayri, *Maktubat-i sadi*, 142. Others name Seth, the third son of Adam and Eve, as the first Sufi: Husayn Va'iz Kashifi, *Futuvatnama-yi sultani*, 41; Hasan Muhammad Chishti, *Majalis-i Hasaniya*, fol. 8b; and Muhammad Gul Ahmadpuri, *Takmila-yi siyar al-awliya'*, 31b.

The method of Sharaf ad-Din Yahya Manayri, *Maktubat-i sadi*, 141.

Hazrat Inayat Khan Inayat Khan, "The Sufi Message" (pamphlet), 1.

130 *Certain early Sufis* S. D. Goitein cites the example of the early Sufi Malik ibn Dinar (d. 744–45), who drew extensively on Jewish sources. *Jews and Arabs*, 149.

I quote also Bahya Ibn Paquda, *The Book of Direction to the Duties of the Heart*, trans. Menahem Mansoor, 11.

The Sufis are See Diana Lobel, *A Sufi-Jewish Dialogue: Philosophy and Mysticism in Bahya Ibn Paquda's Duties of the Heart*.

131 *The Jewish Sufi* 'Obadyah Maimonides, *The Treatise of the Pool*, trans. Paul Fenton, 7.

Abraham Maimonides recognized Abraham Maimonides, *The High Ways to Perfection*, trans. Samuel Rosenblatt, vol. 1, 48–53; vol. 2, 223, 267, 321, 323, and 419.

Inspired by the 'Obadyah Maimonides, *The Treatise of the Pool*, trans. Fenton, 13–17.

132 *Definite Sufi motifs* See Moshe Idel, *Studies in Ecstatic Kabbalah*.

Sarmad! Fame was Muhammad Ahmad Sarmadi, *Tazkira-yi Hazrat Sarmad Shahid*, 69.

I am a Kay Khusraw Isfandiyar, *Dabistan-i mazahib*, vol. 1, 215.

133   *For this reason*   Muhammad Ahmad Sarmadi, *Tazkira-yi Hazrat Sarmad Shahid*, 12.

     My dear friend!   Ibid., 35.

     By means of   'Imran Salahi, *Ru'yaha-yi mard-i nilufari*, 62.

Drop One: Exodus

137   *Master of prophets*   Abraham Maimonides, *The High Ways to Perfection*, trans. Samuel Rosenblatt, vol. 2, 391.

     The Israelites enriched   Exodus 1:7, *The Five Books of Moses*, trans. Robert Alter, 308.

     Miriam, who is   The Zohar (2:12b) calls Miriam "Wisdom" following the Book of Proverbs (7:4).

     The Greatest Shaykh   Ibn 'Arabi, *Fusus al-hikam*, 197; Cf. Louis Ginzberg, *The Legends of the Jews*, vol. 2, 269.

     The basket was   Ibn 'Arabi, *Fusus al-hikam*, 198.

     the tranquility of Sakina   Sakina is the equivalent of the biblical Shekinah.

     A lad weeping   Exodus 2:6, *The Five Books of Moses*, trans. Alter, 313.

     Gabriel had just   Louis Ginzberg, *The Legends of the Jews*, vol. 2, 267.

     Once he cries   The Zohar, trans. Daniel C. Matt, vol. 4, 59.

138   *Moses and Pharaoh*   Rumi, *Masnavi*, 339.

     All the wisdom   Acts 7:22, *The New English Bible*, 155.

Went out to   Exodus 2:11, *The Five Books of Moses*, trans. Alter, 314.

Love for deliverance   Ibn 'Arabi, *Fusus al-hikam*, 203.

The Lord's messenger   Exodus 3:2, *The Five Books of Moses*, trans. Alter, 318.

As the fire   Louis Ginzberg, *The Legends of the Jews*, vol. 2, 303.

Moses, I am   Qur'an 28:30.

Follow the path   Mahmud Shabistari, *Gulshan-i raz*, 21.

139   *Show your white*   Rumi, *Masnavi*, 235.

Come down, O   Muhammad al-Baqi, *'Irfaniyat-i Baqi*, 91.

'Ehyeh-'Asher-'Ehyeh   Exodus 3:14, *The Five Books of Moses*, trans. Alter, 321.

This makes it   Moses Maimonides, *The Guide of the Perplexed*, trans. Shlomo Pines, vol. 2, 155.

Those who come   James L. Kugel, *The Bible as It Was*, 304.

The Greatest Name   Kalim Allah Jahanabadi, *Muraqa'a-yi Kalimi*, 38b. O Living, O Eternal: *Ya Hayy Ya Qayyum*; I-Will-Be-Who-I-Will-Be: *Ahiya Ashir Ahiya*; O Hope of the Hopeful and Helper of the Helpless: *Ay Umid-i Umidvaran o Chara-yi Bicharan*.

Heavy-mouthed and   Exodus 4:11, *The Five Books of Moses*, trans. Alter, 327.

Moses was, and   *The Zohar*, trans. Matt, vol. 4, 91.

Who is the   Exodus 5:1, *The Five Books of Moses*, trans. Alter, 333.

140   *If thou takest*   Qur'an 26:29.

      God in the   Ibn 'Arabi, *Fusus al-hikam*, 198.

      Pharaoh said "I"   Husayn ibn Mansur al-Hallaj,
      Diwan, 158–59; Qur'an 28:38, trans. Arberry, 396.

      The self has   Abu Nasr as-Sarraj, *Kitab al-luma'*,
      430; Qur'an 79:24, trans. Arberry, 628.

      Mansur's "I" was   Rumi, *Masnavi*, 243.

      So he cast   Qur'an 7: 107.

      Moses is religion   Abu'l-Majd Majdud Sana'i,
      Divan, 108.

      The Israelites departed   Exodus 14:9, *The Five
      Books of Moses*, trans. Alter, 392.

141   *For thirty days*   Qur'an 7:142; Exodus 34:28.

      God then added   Muhyi ad-Din Ibn 'Arabi, *The
      Secrets of Voyaging*, trans. Angela Jaffray, 106.

      Hence a retreat   'Umar bin Muhammad
      Suhravardi, *'Awarif al-ma'arif*, vol. 1, 227; 'Ali
      Hujviri, *Kashf al-mahjub*, 418.

      Make solitude   'Abd al-Karim al-Qushayri,
      ar-Risala, 86.

      The principles of   Muhammad Husayni Gisu
      Daraz, *Sharh-i risala-yi Qushayriya*, 439.

      The Sufis of   Abraham Maimonides, *The High
      Ways to Perfection*, trans. Rosenblatt, vol. 2, 415
      and 419 (modified).

      Show me, pray   Exodus 33:17, *The Five Books
      of Moses*, trans. Alter, 505.

      Show me Your   Amir Ahmad Mina'i, *Khiyaban-i
      afrinish va Mahamid-i Khatamunnabiyin*, 138.

      thou shalt not   Qur'an 7:143.

For no human   Exodus 33:20, *The Five Books of Moses*, trans. Alter, 505.

Before the crag   Arini: "Show me"; *Lan tarani*: "Thou shalt not see Me." Mahmud Shabistari, *Gulshan-i raz*, 21.

142   *If you are*   Hadith.

Who could have   Asad Allah Khan Ghalib, *Divan* (Urdu), 25.

So asserts the   Moses Maimonides, *The Guide of the Perplexed*, trans. Pines, vol. 1, 124.

So attests Yeshu'a   James L. Kugel, *The Bible as It Was*, 375.

Illuminated by the   *The Zohar*, trans. Matt, vol. 5, 584, note 91.

Mount Sinai started   Rumi, *Masnavi*, 37.

If with that   Farid ad-Din 'Attar, *Musibatnama*, 345.

Moses's wrath flared: Exodus 32:28, *The Five Books of Moses*, trans. Alter, 499.

143   *A drought struck*   Muhammad al-Ghazali, *Ihya' 'ulum ad-din*, vol. 5, 59–60.

I have assigned   Rumi, *Masnavi*, 216.

Do not take   Ibid., 217.

144   *meeting of the*   Qur'an 18:60.

knowledge proceeding from   Ibid., 18:65.

Khizr agreed to   Ahmad Maybudi, *Tafsir-i adabi va 'irfani-yi Qur'an-i majid*, vol. 2, 18–19; Qur'an 89:27.

If you'd have   Asad Allah Khan Ghalib, *Divan* (Farsi), 315.

But no prophet   Deuteronomy 34:10, *The Five Books of Moses*, trans. Alter, 1059.

Drop Two: Ascent in Song

147   *And water will*   Exodus 17:6, *The Five Books of Moses*, trans. Alter, 413.

And there gushed   Qur'an 2:60.

Each fountain, as   Gabriel Attias and Gaston-Paul Effa, *Le Juif et l'Africain*, 120.

And from Your   Psalm 36:9, *The Book of Psalms*, trans. Robert Alter, 127.

God has not   Hadith.

148   *O you mountains*   Qur'an 34:10.

The mountain with   Rumi, *Masnavi*, 453.

It was the   *The Zohar*, trans. Matt, vol. 4, 374.

Acclaim the Lord   Psalm 33:2–3, *The Book of Psalms*, trans. Alter, 113.

O strummer of   Jamal ad-Din Jamman, *Muntakhaba-yi divan*, 21.

How can I   'Abd al-Karim al-Qushayri, *ar-Risala*, 138.

Once, it is   Perek Shirah, trans. Rabbi Natan Slifkin, 21.

Solomon's songs numbered   1 Kings 5:12.

149   *And no human*   *The Zohar*, trans. Matt, vol. 5, 321.

The whole world   Ibid., vol. 5, 314, note 350.

Am I not   Qur'an 7:172.

I saw all   Gisu Daraz, *Javahir al-'ushshaq*, 36.

I don't know   Nur al-Hasan Sahasvani, *Naghmat-i sama'*, 228.

Hymns rang out   1 Chronicles 23:5.

My friend, there   Allahdiya Chishti, *Siyar al-aqtab*, 75.

In the religion   Mas'ud Bakk, *Divan*, 161.

150   *Music's detractor is*   Inayat Khan, *Inayat git ratnavali*, v.

The Proof of   Muhammad al-Ghazali, *Ihya' 'ulum ad-din*, vol. 2, 335.

To bring forth   Ibid., 332.

When the Messenger   Shams ad-Din Ahmad Aflaki, *Manaqib al-'arifin*, vol. 1, 482–83.

Infinite Thou, and   Raymond P. Scheindlin, *The Gazelle*, 177.

Drop Three: A David Psalm

153   *You fathom my*   Psalm 139:2, *The Book of Psalms*, trans. Alter, 479.

God knows the   Qur'an 3:119.

From behind and   Psalm 139:5, *The Book of Psalms*, trans. Alter, 480.

God created the   Genesis 1:27, *The Five Books of Moses*, trans. Alter, 19 (modified).

God created us   Rumi, *Masnavi*, 520.

When the blessed   *The Zohar*, trans. Matt, vol. 1, 236, note 1036 (citing Genesis 1:27).

154   *Behind and in*   *The Zohar*, trans. Matt, vol. 4, 284–85 (2:55a). Some Sufis conceive of the original human as Eve, and say that Adam was

created from the body of Eve. They adduce evidence from the verse, *Mankind, fear your Lord, who Created you of a single soul, and from it created its mate, and from the pair of them scattered abroad many men and women* (Qur'an 4:1). Here, a single soul (*nafsin wahidatin*) is grammatically feminine and its mate (*zawjaha*) is masculine. Muhammad Nasir 'Andalib, *Nala-yi 'Andalib*, 445.

I have created Ahmad Maybudi, *Tafsir-i adabi va 'irfani-yi Qur'an-i majid*, vol. 1, 180.

When man and Rumi, *Masnavi*, 71.

Darkness itself will Psalm 139:12, *The Book of Psalms*, trans. Alter, 481.

Night and day *The Zohar*, trans. Matt, vol. 1, 195.

Don't sleep, my 'Attar, *Musibatnama*, 254.

Though he walk Isaiah 50:10, *The Prophets: Nevi'im*, 471.

155 *My night is* Shahab ad-Din Ahmad Sam'ani, *Rawh al-arvah fi sharh asma' al-Malik al-Fattah*, 172.

The days were Psalm 139:16, *The Book of Psalms*, trans. Alter, 482.

Remind Thou them Qur'an 14:5; Ahmad Maybudi, *Tafsir-i adabi va irfani-yi Qur'an-i majid*, vol. 1, 516.

Is it not Ahmad Ghazali, *Majmu'a-yi asar-i Farsi*, 169.

Those primordial days Psalm 104:16, *The Book of Psalms*, trans. Alter, 365; *The Zohar*, trans. Matt, vol. 1, 190.

So great is *The Zohar*, trans. Matt, vol. 1, 192,

note 688.

We are mere Amir Ahmad Mina'i, *Divan*, 198.

156   *Enoch on Sunday* Muhyi ad-Din Ibn 'Arabi, *Mawaqi' an-nujum*, 171–72.

Every day He Qur'an 55:29.

Do not curse Hadith.

Search me, God Psalm 139:20, *The Book of Psalms*, trans. Alter, 483.

Surely God is Qur'an 33:55.

O Lord, I Amir Hasan Dihlavi, *Divan*, 581–82.

Drop Four: Job

159   *On the second day* *The Zohar*, trans. Matt, vol. 5, 196.

He goes down Joseph ben Abraham Gikatilla, *Sha'are orah*, trans. Avi Weinstein, 213.

He has also 'Ayn al-Quzat Hamadani, *Tamhidat*, 74. Cf. Ruzbihan Baqli, *Sharh-i shathiyat*, 510.

He leads astray Qur'an 16:93.

Surely unto God Ibid., 42:53.

I am enamored Rumi, *Masnavi*, 63.

And yet, reach Job 1:11, *The Wisdom Books*, trans. Robert Alter, 13.

160   *When Shibli was* al-Qushayri, *ar-Risala*, 146.

You incited Me Job 2:3, *The Wisdom Books*, trans. Alter, 15.

And he took Ibid., Job 2:8, 15.

Surely we found Qur'an 38:44.

Shall we accept   Job 2:10, *The Wisdom Books*, trans. Alter, 16.

This is the   Joseph ben Abraham Gikatilla, *Sha'are orah*, trans. Weinstein, 213.

Would that I   Job 23:3, *The Wisdom Books*, trans. Alter, 98.

161   *The Proof of*   Muhammad al-Ghazali, *Kimiya as-sa'adat*, 53.

How can man   Job 9:2–4, *The Wisdom Books*, trans. Alter, 42.

At the court   Rumi, *Masnavi*, 467.

Behold, affliction has   Ibid., 21:83.

My skin turned   Job 30–31, *The Wisdom Books*, trans. Alter, 126.

God drew forth   al-Qushayri, *ar-Risala*, 147.

162   *those who hurt*   Qur'an 33:57.

"Then" says the   Ibn 'Arabi, *Fusus al-hikam*, 174.

The object of   'Attar, *Ilahinama*, 404.

Where were you   Job 38:4, *The Wisdom Books*, trans. Alter, 158.

By the ear's   Job 42:4–6, *The Wisdom Books*, trans. Alter, 177.

Ever modest before   Rumi, *Masnavi*, 770.

Wave Five: the Messiah's Breath

165   *It is related*   al-Qushayri, *ar-Risala*, 271.

If with a   Ibn 'Arabi, *Tarjuman al-ashwaq*, 18.

When I was   'Attar, *Divan*, 421.

Should Venus intone   Shams ad-Din Muhammad Hafiz, *Divan*, 72.

According to Sufi   Husayn Va'iz Kashifi, *Futuvatnama-yi sultani*, 117.

166   *Many years later*   Muhammad ibn Ishaq, *The Life of Muhammad*, trans. Alfred Guillaume, 107. Bahira and Waraqa may have regarded Muhammad as the parakletos predicted in John 14:16, an identification later made by several Muslim commentators.

Of a truth   Muhammad ibn Ishaq, *The Life of Muhammad*, trans. Guillaume, 152.

Some of them   Qur'an 5:82.

The early Sufis   See Tor Andrae, *In the Garden of Myrtles: Studies in Early Islamic Mysticism*, trans. Birgitta Sharpe.

It is often   'Ali Hujviri, *Kashf al-mahjub*, 34.

The Kethabha dhe-yauna   A. J. Wensinck, *Bar Hebraeus's Book of the Dove*, Introduction.

167   *The Majorcan polymath*   Anthony Bonner, *Doctor Illuminatus*, 189.

Intriguing commonalities exist   Miguel Asin Palacios, *Islam and the Divine Comedy*, trans. Harold Sutherland, 42–54.

Sufi symbols saturate   Luce López-Baralt, "Saint John of the Cross and Ibn 'Arabi."

And in recent   Pope Francis, *Laudato si'*, 175–76.

The Passion of al-Hallaj, trans. Mason, vol. 3, 219–21.

I am the John 15:6.

I will die al-Hallaj, *Diwan*, 67.

168 *Other Sufis may* Louis Massignon, *The Passion of al-Hallaj*, trans. Mason, vol. 2, 166–69; Claudia Liebeskind, *Piety on Its Knees*, 185–86; Michel Chodkiewicz, *Seal of the Saints*, trans. Liadain Sherrard, 83.

they did not Qur'an 4:157.

In the throes Todd Lawson, *The Crucifixion and the Qur'an*, 4.

has not begotten Qur'an 112:1.

169 *My Beloved is* Ibn 'Arabi, *Tarjuman al-ashwaq*, trans. R. A. Nicholson, 70–71.

Concerning the Essence Reynold Alleyne Nicholson, *Studies in Islamic Mysticism*, 104.

Shabistari identifies the Mahmud Shabistari, *Gulshan-i raz*, 96.

Therefore Jesus said Ibid, 97.

170 *In a church* Hatif Isfahani, *Divan*, 48–49. Cf. Evagrius Ponticus's contention that the Trinity is not a mathematical triad in *Kephalaia Gnostika*, trans. Ilaria Ramelli, 321–23.

I had accompanied Sirkar van Stolk, *Memories of a Sufi Sage*, 65–67.

Drop One: Our Lady

175 *Truly God provisions* Qur'an 3:37.

The goal of Gregory of Nyssa, *Ascetical Works*, 42.

The Speaker urged Exodus 19:15.

How swift, O   Ephrem the Syrian, *Hymns*, trans. Kathleen McVey, 271.

boy most pure   Qur'an 19:19.

With God nothing   Luke 1:37, *New English Bible*, 69, note c.

176   *I am the*   Ibid., 1:38.

From Mary's water   Ibn 'Arabi, *Fusus al-hikam*, 138.

The virgin earth   Ephrem the Syrian, *Hymns*, trans. McVey, 65.

In this world   Abu'l-Majd Majdud Sana'i, *Hadiqat al-haqiqat*, 185.

The baby stirred   Luke 1:41, *New English Bible*, 69.

When I came   Rumi, *Masnavi*, 282.

177   *Kindness and truth*   Psalm 85:11, *The Book of Psalms*, trans. Alter, 301.

The one you   *The Nag Hammadi Scriptures*, ed. Marvin Meyer, 496.

they did not   Qur'an 4:157.

Observe that, in   Ruzbihan Baqli Shirazi, *Sharh-i shathiyat*, 46-7.

At the close   Philotheus, *The History of the Blessed Virgin Mary*, trans. E. A. Wallis Budge, 109-115.

178   *The holy Mother*   Inayat Khan, *Diwan*, 23.

Drop Two: The Word

181   *A brother came*   *The Desert Fathers*, trans. Benedicta Ward, 20.

its roots are   Qur'an 14:24.

Wherever generosity's tree   Muslih Sa'di, *Kulliyat*, 155.

uprooted from the   Qur'an 14:26.

Out of your   Matthew 12:37, *New English Bible*, 18.

Only when you   'Attar, *Ilahinama*, 299.

182   *Speak the truth*   Ephesians 4:25, *New English Bible*, 248.

The Spirit passed   Tarif Khalidi, *The Muslim Jesus*, 96.

God's own Word   Qur'an 4:171.

When all things   John 1:1, *New English Bible*, 110.

Because he is   'Attar, *Ilahinama*, 130.

those that outstrip   Qur'an 79:4.

those that direct   Ibid, 79:5.

Not on bread   Deuteronomy 8:4, *The Five Books of Moses*, trans. Alter, 921–22.

When he decrees   Qur'an 2:117.

183   *The lesser words*   Shahab ad-Din Yahya Suhravardi, *Majmu'a-yi asar-i Farsi-yi Shaykh-i Ishraq*, vol. 3, 216–23.

A man who   Evagrius Ponticus, *The Praktikos and Chapters on Prayer*, trans. John Eudes Bamberger, 39.

Receive the Holy   John 20:22, *New English Bible*, 142.

O sweet breeze   Shams ad-Din Muhammad Hafiz, *Divan*, 103.

By the Word   Psalm 33:6, *The Book of Psalms*, trans. Alter, 114.

All is in   Ibn 'Arabi, *Fusus al-hikam*, 145.

184   *Purity is the*   Isaac the Syrian, *The Ascetical Homilies*, trans. The Holy Transfiguration Monastery, 468.

Drop Three: Purification

184   *The way of Jesus*   Rumi, *Fihi ma fih*, 87.

There is joy   Luke 15:10, *New English Bible*, 95.

As Abba Isaac: Isaac of Nineveh, *Mystic Treatises*, trans. A.J. Wensinck, 7.

At every step   'Ayn al-Quzat Hamadani, *Namaha*, vol. 2, 256.

On the feet   Muslih Sa'di, *Kulliyat*, 295.

188   *Surely life is*   Matthew 6:25, *New English Bible*, 10.

Fasting is the   John Climacus, *The Ladder of Divine Ascent*, trans. Colm Luibheid and Norman Russell, 169.

Hunger is a   Muhammad al-Ghazali, *Ihya' 'ulum ad-din*, vol. 3, 105.

An untainted inwardness   Muslih Sa'di, *Kulliyat* 296.

That nature sets   Galatians 5:17, *New English Bible*, 243.

Whoever stirs up   Muslih Sa'di, *Kulliyat*, 296.

189   *Avarice suggests to*   Evagrius Ponticus, *The Praktikos and Chapters on Prayers*, trans. Bamberger, 17.

Do not be   Matthew 6:34, *New English Bible*, 10.

Come! Let's forget   Sadiq Hidayat, *Taranaha-yi Khayyam*, 108.

Do not occupy   'Ali Hujviri, *Kashf al-mahjub*, 480.

Whether you strive Muslih Sa'di, *Kulliyat*, 168.

The very days Sadiq Hidayat, *Taranaha-yi Khayyam*, 108.

190 *When you blasted* Rumi, *Masnavi*, 423.

The Messenger said Hadith.

Anyone who nurses Matthew 5:22, *New English Bible*, 7.

Do not let Ephesians 4:26, *New English Bible*, 248.

Though the charge Nur al-Hasan Sahasvani, *Naghmat-i sama'*, 354.

191 *Fortify me, O* Muslih Sa'di, *Kulliyat*, 89.

The cat keeps John Climacus, *The Ladder of Divine Ascent*, trans. Luibheid and Russell, 262.

Shibli learned the Muhammad Mubarak Kirmani, *Siyar al-awliya'*, 448.

The greed of 'Abd al-Qadir Bidil, *Divan*, 229.

A monk was John Climacus, *The Ladder of Divine Ascent*, trans. Luibheid and Russell, 204–5.

192 *You fell when* Bu 'Ali Shah Qalandar, *Divan*, 256.

If pride turned John Climacus, *The Ladder of Divine Ascent*, trans. Luibheid and Russell, 227.

To the humble Isaac of Nineveh, *Mystic Treatises*, trans. Wensinck, 36.

On this threshold Muslih Sa'di, *Kulliyat*, 267.

Whoever exalts himself Matthew 23:12, *New English Bible*, 32.

193 *My words and* Muhsin Fayz Kashani, *Divan-i kamil*, 642.

My sins are Muhammad Ahmad Sarmadi, *Tazkira-yi Hazrat Sarmad Shahid*, 62.

As my sins Amir Ahmad Mina'i, *Divan*, 218.

Drop Four: Illumination

197 *Bar 'Ibraya enumerates* Bar Hebraeus, *The Book of the Dove*, trans. Wensinck, 56–58, 110–13.

Spiritual knowledge is Isaac of Ninevah, *Mystic Treatises*, trans. Wensinck, 354.

Abraham of Nathpar Sebastian Brock, *The Syriac Fathers on Prayer and the Spiritual Life*, 195.

The Spirit instructed Matthew 18:3, *New English Bible*, 25.

198 *When the mind* Hierotheos (att.), *The Book of the Holy Hierotheos*, trans. F. S. Marsh, 38.

I am setting Qur'an 2:30.

In Christ He Ephesians 1:4, *New English Bible*, 245.

We are the Muhammad Munir ad-Din Mahmudi, *Shajarat al-Mahmud*, 156.

The Kingdom of Luke 17:21, *New English Bible*, 98, note a.

Hajji Imdad Allah Imdad Allah Muhajir Makki, *Ziya' al-qulub*, 77.

But as Gregory Gregory the Great, *Moralia in Job*, vol. 1, 13.

199 *Bar 'Ibraya explains* Bar Hebraeus, *Book of the Dove*, trans. Wensinck, 57.

Tears keep erupting Muhammad Taqi Niyazi, *Raz-i niyaz*, 81.

Mas'ud Bakk's tears 'Abd ar-Rahman Chishti, *Mirat al-asrar*, trans. Wahidbakhsh Siyal Chishti, 1019.

To see mystically Amir Ahmad Mina'i, *Divan*, 156.

It is the Isaac the Syrian, *The Ascetical Homilies*, trans. Holy Transfiguration, 491.

Pray first for Evagrius Ponticus, T*he Praktikos and Chapters on Prayer*, trans. Bambeger, 56.

Hot tears and Siraj ad-Din Siraj Awrangabadi, *Kulliyat*, 126.

The Creation is Hadith.

200 *O Lord, on* Muhammad bin Munavvar, *Asrar at-tawhid*, vol. 1, 227.

I could even Romans 9:3, *New English Bible*, 200.

from the shadows Qur'an 5:16.

I have thrown The Gospel of Thomas 10, T*he Nag Hammadi Scriptures*, ed. Meyer, 140.

Our God is *Writings from the Philokalia on the Prayer of the Heart*, trans. E. Kadloubovsky and G. E. H. Palmer, 76.

God Himself is Pseudo-Dionysius, *The Complete Works*, trans. Colm Luibheid,178. Cf. Evagrius Ponticus, *Kephalaia Gnostika*, trans. Ramelli, 32.

Dionysius advises the Pseudo-Dionysius, *The Complete Works*, trans. Luibheid, 68.

The Master of Shahab ad-Din Yahya Suhravardi, *Majmu'a-yi musannafat*, vol. 1, 108.

201 *Born of breath* Mas'ud Bakk, *Divan*, 153.

The voices of Bar Hebraeus, T*he Book of the Dove*, trans. Wensinck, 57.

As the Shaykh   Kalim Allah Jahanabadi, *Kashkul-i Kalimi*, 37.

When I gave   Muhsin Fayz Kashani, *Divan-i kamil*, 605.

Choked by cares   Luke 8:14, *New English Bible*, 82.

Your divine beauty   Gregory of Nyssa, *From Glory to Glory*, trans. Jean Daniélou, 101.

The righteous will   Matthew 13:43, *New English Bible*, 20.

The desert father   Isaac of Nineveh, *Mystic Treatises*, trans. Wensinck, 377.

202   *It is said*   Rashid ad-Din Mawdud Lala, *Mukhbir al-awliya'*, fol. 479b.

Prayer is terminated   Isaac of Nineveh, *Mystic Treatises*, trans. Wensinck, 118.

The power of   Luke 1:35, *New English Bible*, 69.

When I love   Hadith Qudsi.

My qualities became   Muhammad Riza Shafi'i Kadkani, *Daftar-i rawshanayi*, 306–7.

Miserable is the   Qutb ad-Din Bakhtiyar Kaki (att.), *Divan*, 58.

203   *The mind only*   Bar Hebraeus, *The Book of the Dove*, trans. Wensinck, 57.

What is there   Mas'ud Bakk, *Divan*, 155.

The guarded tablet   Qur'an 85:22.

A blessing to   Ephesians 4:29, *New English Bible*, 248.

If I tell The Gospel of Thomas 8, in *The Nag Hammadi Scriptures*, Ed. Meyer, 141.

When the shaykh 'Attar, *Tazkirat al-awliya'*, 204.

Drop Five: The Robe of Glory

207   *When I was* The Acts of Thomas 108:1–3, trans. Harold Attridge, 84.

If you descend Ibid., 108:12–15, 85.

208   *You have seen* Rumi, *Masnavi*, 191.

One day when 'Attar, *Tazkirat al-awliya'*, 126–27.

209   *Ibn Sirin says* Muhammad ibn Sirin, *Tafsir al-ahlam*, 144.

Your greatest enemy Hadith.

The ego is hell Rumi, *Masnavi*, 56.

I forgot I The Acts of Thomas 109:33–35, trans. Attridge, 86-7.

The water of Pistis Sophia, trans. G. R. S. Mead, 320.

This world's oblivion Ahmad Mina'i, *Khiyaban-i afrinish va Mahamid-i Khatamunnabiyin*, 239.

Awake and rise The Acts of Thomas 110:41–46, trans. Attridge, 87.

210   *What do you* Rumi, *Masnavi*, 188.

The pearl that Muhammad Ziya' al-Hasan Jili Kalimi, *Kalam-i Ziya'*, 105.

Against the little soul Rumi, *Masnavi*, 196.

211   *Those who went* Muhammad Husayni Gisu Daraz, *Wujud al-'ashiqin*, 8.

When you strip The Gospel of Thomas 37 in *The Nag Hammadi Scriptures*, ed. Meyer, 144.

Raiment of dawn Shahab ad-Din Yahya
Suhravardi, *Majmu'a-yi musannafat*, vol. 2, 503.

Suddenly, when I The Acts of Thomas 112:76–78,
trans. Attridge, 89.

212   *This son of* Luke 15:24, *New English Bible*, 95.

Many are the Muhammad Tahir Ghani, *Divan*, 35.

Wave Six: The Seal of Prophecy

215   *I am the* Jalal ad-Din Rumi, *Taranaha-yi
shurangiz*, 221.

I tell you Nur al-Hasan Sahasvani, *Naghmat-i
sama'*, 228.

I will ask John 14:16, *New English Bible*, 132.

a messenger who Qur'an 61:6.

I am Ahad Hadith.

He taught that Origen, *On First Principles*,
trans. Henri De Lubac, 116.

216   *When the Divine* Muhammad Taqi Niyazi,
Raz-i takhliq, 5–6.

217   *Each prophet had* Inayat Khan, *The Sufi Message*,
vol. 5, 20.

When you take Rumi, *Masnavi*, 62.

218   *Whoever partakes of* Ibid., 721.

Sufi theologians add See the chapter on Ezra
in Ibn al-'Arabi, *Fusus al-hikam*.

Root of all Letter to Rabia Martin dated 27 July
1913.

They say that Rumi, *Fihi ma fih*, 128.

219   *Once 'Ali, may*   Hamid Qalandar, *Khayr al-majalis*, 128–29. Cf. Muhammad Husayni Gisu Daraz, *Majmu'a-yi yazda rasa'il*, 122.

    And do not   Qur'an 6:52.

    Be of good   Rashid ad-Din Maybudi, *Tafsir-i adabi va 'irfani-yi Qur'an-i majid*, vol. 1, 286.

220   *Having received spiritual*   *Risala-yi chahar o chaharda khanvada*, 1b.

    In this manner   An exception to the otherwise universal derivation of Sufi lineages through 'Ali is the Naqshbandi lineage, which is traced through Abu Bakr.

    Today Sufism is   'Ali Hujviri, *Kashf al-mahjub*, 4–9.

Drop One: Bearing Witness

223   *Outward, the Inward*   Qur'an 57:3 and 1:1.

    Were there gods   Ibid., 21:22.

    How long will   Sharaf ad-Din Manayri, *Maktubat-i sadi*, 30.

224   *There is no*   Qur'an 47:19.

    Beholding Your works   Abu'l-Majd Majdud Sana'i, *Divan*, 385.

    With certainty they   'Abd al-Karim al-Qushayri, *ar-Risala*, 88.

225   *remember Me, and*   Qur'an 2:152.

    If the connection   Ahmad Ghazali, *Majmu'a-yi asar-i* Farsi, 135.

    There is no   Husayn Va'iz Kashifi, *Rashahat*, 181. Cf. Muhammad Dara Shikuh, *Hasanat* al-'arifin, trans. Muhammad 'Umar Khan, 6.

Our only song Asad Allah Khan Ghalib,
Divan (Farsi), 101.

Someone asked Sa'd 'Aziz ad-Din Nasafi,
Kashf al-haqa'iq, 153.

knowledge of certainty Qur'an 102:5, 102:7, 56:95.

226   *Union is a* Gisu Daraz, *Javahir al-'ushshaq*, 29.

On the Day Muhammad Riza Shafi'i Kadkani,
Nivishta bar darya, 275.

Selfishness is faithlessness 'Aziz ad-Din Nasafi,
Kashf al-haqa'iq, 170.

Drop Two: Prayer

229   *two-bows'-length* Qur'an 53:9.

God enjoined the Muhammad ibn Hisham, *The
Life of Muhammad*, trans. Guillaume, 186–87.

Each the five Ahmad Maybudi, *Tafsir-i adabi
va 'irfani-yi Qur'an-i majid*, 99–100.

230   *There is no* Hadith.

When I am Kalim Allah Jahanabadi, *Kashkul-i
Kalimi*, 6.

A fool once 'Attar, *Ilahinama*, 187.

A prayer performed Abu'l-Majd Majdud Sana'i,
Hadiqat al-haqiqat va shari'at at-tariqat, 141.

231   *Ablution is separation* 'Ayn al-Quzat Hamadani,
Tamhidat, 79.

The Shaykh of Sharaf ad-Din Manayri,
Maktubat-i sadi, 200.

I see Your Hasan Sijzi Dihlavi, *Divan*, 88.

The Lion of Muhammad Ghazali, *Ihya' 'ulum ad-din*, vol. 1, 206; Qur'an 33:72.

232 *Each one of* Hadith.

Lord of all Qur'an 1:1-4.

Sincerity is to Hadith.

This is the Muhammad Taqi Niyazi, *Raz-i Niyaz*, 23.

Union with the Mu'in ad-Din Chishti (att.), *Mutarjam maktub*, 31.

Drop Three: Almsgiving

235 *Once it happened* 'Ali Hujviri, *Kashf al-mahjub*, 408.

Why should the Muslih Sa'di, *Kulliyat*, 231.

Surely, Abraham was Qur'an 16:120, (modified).

The Martyr of Louis Massignon, *The Passion of al-Hallaj*, trans. Mason, vol. 1, 122.

Become a Hanif Mahmud Shabistari, *Gulshan-i raz*, 99.

236 *Ibn Ishaq tells* Muhammad ibn Ishaq, *The Life of Muhammad*, trans. Guillaume, 105.

Someone buries an Shams ad-Din Aflaki, *Manaqib al-'arifin*, vol. 1, 304.

The hand that Rumi, *Masnavi*, 422.

To test his Sharaf ad-Din Manayri, *Maktubat-i sadi*, 210.

237 *Abu Bakr the* Muhammad al-Ghazali, *Ihya' 'ulum ad-din*, vol. 1, 288.

Give whenever you Ziya' ad-Din Nakhshabi, *Silk as-suluk*, 76.

It was the   Muhammad al-Ghazali, *Ihya' 'ulum
ad-din*, vol. 1, 304; Qur'an 3:86, (modified).

The Sufi is   'Ali Hujviri, *Kashf al-mahjub*, 42.

Alms fall into   Hadith.

Last night while   'Attar, *Tazkirat al-awliya'*, 172.

Drop Four: Fasting

241   *say, 'I have*   Qur'an 19:26.

    The fire of   Ahmad Maybudi, *Tafsir-i adabi va
'irfani-yi Qur'an-i majid*, vol. 1, 74.

    If He burns   Ibid.

    Half of patience   Hadith.

    Half of the   'Ali Hujviri, *Kashf al-mahjub*, 413.

242   *God made the*   Ahmad Maybudi, *Tafsir-i adabi
va 'irfani-yi Qur'an-i majid*, vol. 1, 74.

    feeds and is   Qur'an 6:14.

    The believer is   Rumi, *Masnavi*, 948.

    What sweetness hides   Jalal ad-Din Rumi *Kulliyat-i
Shams*, vol. 4, 68.

    Like Him there   Qur'an 42:11.

    Fasting is absenting   'Ayn al-Quzat Hamadani,
Tamhidat, 91.

    Rid the road   Inayat Khan, *Minqar-i musiqar*, 153.

    For the one   Hadith.

243   *The fast is*   Hadith Qudsi.

    'Ayn al-Quzat says   'Ayn al-Quzat Hamadani,
Tamhidat, 91, alluding to the Hadith, "I pass the

night with my Lord, and he gives me food and drink," and Qur'an 42:11.

O Sublime Defender   Muhammad Husayni Gisu Daraz, *Javahir al-'ushshaq*, 24.

To fast from   Shams ad-Din Ahmad Aflaki, *Manaqib al-'arifin*, vol. 1, 280.

Drop Five: Pilgrimage

247   *Every Hajj you*   'Attar, *Musibat nama*, 396.

248   *in the horizons*   Qur'an 41:53.

Journey in themselves   Ibid.

If he is   Qur'an 3:97; 'Aziz ad-Din Nasafi, *Kashf al-haqa'iq*, 228–29.

I have turned   Qur'an 6:79 (modified).

The Shaykh of   'Ali Hujviri, *Kashf al-mahjub*, 424.

The world is   Gisu Daraz, *Javahir al-'ushshaq*, 29.

In the pilgrimage   'Ali Hujviri, *Kashf al-mahjub*, 427.

Pilgrims circumambulate the   Muhammad Mubarak Kirmani, *Siyar al-awliya'*, 45.

249   *I was in*   Ahmad Maybudi, *Tafsir-i adabi va 'irfani-yi Qur'an-i majid*, vol. 1, 80.

The Shaykha of   'Attar, *Tazkirat al-awliya'*, 90.

It wasn't love   Sharaf ad-Din Manayri, *Maktubat-i sadi*, 107.

The human heart   Mu'in ad-Din Chishti (att.), *Maktubat*, 58.

I have not   Gisu Daraz, *Javahir al-'ushshaq*, 12.

Without us He Gisu Daraz, *Javahir al-'ushshaq*, 12.

The Shaykh of 'Ayn al-Quzat Hamadani, *Tamhidat*, 94. A different version appears in Farid ad-Din 'Attar, *Tazkirat al-awliya'*, 203.

250 *There was a* Muhammad Mubarak Kirmani, *Siyar al-awliya'*, 45.

Don't bemoan the Gisu Daraz, *Wujud al-'ashiqin*, 14.

Conclusion

253 *One whose footstep* Muhammad Tahir Ghani, *Divan*, 30.

Wave, drop, or bubble Jamal ad-Din Jamman, *Muntakhaba-yi divan*, 2.

Ma'ruf Karkhi showed Husayn Mu'izz Balkhi in Sharaf ad-Din Manayri, *Maktubat-i sadi*, 200.

When Kabir died Kabir, *Kabir dohavali*, 46.

All the religious Shams ad-Din Ahmad Aflaki, *Manaqib al-'arifin*, vol. 2, 592.

254 *Whoever is occupied* Muhammad Dara Shikuh, *Hasanat al-'arifin*, trans. Khan, 23.

To be of Abu'l-Majd Majdud Sana'i, *Divan*, 1008.

255 *Contempt and esteem* Muhammad Dara Shikuh, *Hasanat al-'arifin*, trans. Khan, 23.

The real infidel Jamal ad-Din Jamman, *Divan*, 7.

On the Day Rumi, *Fihi ma fih*, 215.

In love there Sharaf ad-Din Manayri, *Maktubat-i sadi*, 200.

Watered with one   Qur'an 13:4.

256   *As you are*   Muhammad Nasir 'Andalib, *Nala-yi 'Andalib*, vol. 2, 450. 63.

Bibliography

'Abd al-Karim ibn Hawazin al-Qushayri, Shaykh. *ar-Risala al-Qushayriya*. Cairo: Muhammad 'Ali Subayh, 1966.

'Abd al-Qadir Bidil, Mawlana. *Divan*. Ed. Husayn Ahi. Tehran: Furughi, 1992–93.

———. *Shu'la-avaz: Masnaviha*. Ed. Akbar Bihdarvand. Tehran: Mu'assasa-yi Intisharat-i Nigah, 2009–10.

'Abd ar-Rahman Chishti. *Mirat al-asrar*. Trans. Wahid-bakhsh Siyal Chishti. Delhi: Maktaba-yi Jam-i Nur, 1997.

'Abd ar-Rahman as-Sulami. *Tabaqat as-sufiya*. Ed. Nur ad-Din Surayba. Cairo: Maktabat al-Khanji, 1986.

'Abd ar-Razzaq Kashani. *Istilahat as-sufiya*. Trans. Muhammad Khvajavi. Tehran: Intisharat-i Mawla, 1993.

Abraham Maimonides. *The High Ways to Perfection*. Trans. Samuel Rosenblatt. 2 vols. New York: Columbia University Press, 1927, and Baltimore: The Johns Hopkins Press, 1938.

Abu Bakr Muhammad ibn Ishaq al-Kalabadhi. *at-Ta'aruf li-madhhab ahl at-tasawwuf*. Beirut: Dar al-Kutub al-'Ilmiya, 1993.

Abu Hamid Muhammad al-Ghazali, Shaykh. *Ihya' 'ulum ad-din*. Ed. 'Abd al-Mu'ti Amin Qala'aji. 5 vols. Beirut: Dar Sadir, 2010.

———. *Kimiya as-sa'adat*. Tehran: Kitabkhana wa Chapkhna-yi Markazi, 1940–41.

———. *Mishkat al-anwar*. Ed. Abu'l-'Ala 'Afifi. Cairo: Ad Dar al-Qawmiya, 1964.

Abu Nasr as-Sarraj. *Kitab al-luma'*. Cairo and Baghdad: Dar al-Kutub al-Haditha and Maktabat al-Mithanna, 1960.

Abu'l-Fayz Fayzi. *Divan*. Ed. A.D. Arshad. Tehran: Intisharat-i Furughi, 1983–84.

Abu'l-Fazl 'Allami. *A'in-i Akbari*. Trans. H. Blochmann. Calcutta: The Asiatic Society of Bengal, 1927.

Abu'l-Qasim Firdawsi. *Shahnama*. Ed. Jalal Khaliqi Mutlaq. 8 vols. New York: Bibliotheca Persica, 1988–2008.

Abu'l-Majd Majdud Sana'i, Hakim. *Divan*. Ed. Mudarris Razavi. Tehran: Intisharat-i Sana'i, 1983–84.

———. *Hadiqat al-haqiqat wa shari'at at-tariqa*t. Ed. Mudarris Razavi. Tehran: Instisharat-i Danishgah-i Tihran, 2015.

The Acts of Thomas. Trans. Harold W. Attridge. Salem, OR: Polebridge Press, 2010.

Ahmad Ghazali, Shaykh. *Majmu'a-yi asar-i Farsi*. Ed. Ahmad Mujahid. Tehran: Intisharat-i Danishgah-i Tihran, 1979.

Ahmad Jam, Shaykh. *Divan*. Ed. Ahmad Karami. Tehran: Nashriyat-i Ma, 1986.

Ahmad Maybudi, Imam. *Khulasa-yi tafsir-i adabi va 'irfani-yi Qur'an-i majid*. 2 vols. Tehran: Iqbal, 2014–15.

Ahmad Mina'i, Amir. *Divan*. Lucknow: Matba'-yi Naval Kishur, 1922.

———. *Khiyaban-i afrinish va Mahamid-i Khatamunnabi-yin*. Ed. Isra'il Ahmad Mina'i. Karachi: Paramount Publishing, 2010.

Ahmad Shah Chishti Mawdudi, Sayyid. *Nava-yi Chishtiyan*. Herat: Intisharat-i Ahrari, 2012.

Akbar Hadi. *Sharh-i hal-i Mir Damad va Mir Findiriski ba-inzimam-i divan-i Mir Damad va qasida-yi Mir Findiriski.* Isfahan: Intisharat-i Maysam Tammar, 1964.

Akbar Husayni, Sayyid. *Tabsirat al-istilahat as-sufiya.* Hyderabad: Mu'in Press, 1946.

Allahdiya Chishti. *Siyar al-aqtab.* Lucknow: Naval Kishur, 1889.

'Ali ibn 'Usman Hujviri, Shaykh. *Kashf al-mahjub.* Tehran: Amir Kabir, 1957.

Andrae, Tor. *In the Garden of Myrtles: Studies in Early Islamic Mysticism.* Trans. Birgitta Sharpe. Albany: State University of New York Press, 1987.

Arberry, Arthur John. *The Koran Interpreted.* Oxford: Oxford University Press, 1964.

Asad Allah Khan Ghalib, Mirza. *Divan* (Urdu). New Delhi: Ghalib Institute, 1986.

———. *Divan* (Farsi). Ed. Muhammad Hasan Ha'iri. Tehran: Miras-i Maktub, 2006.

Ashva-ghosha. *Life of the Buddha.* Trans. Patrick Olivelle. New York: New York University Press, 2008.

Attias, Gabriel, and Effa, Gaston-Paul. *Le Juif et l'Africain: Double Offrande.* Monaco: Éditions du Rocher, 2003.

Aturpat-i Emetan. *The Wisdom of the Sasanian Sages* (Denkart VI). Trans. Shaul Shaked. Boulder: Westview Press, 1979.

'Ayn al-Quzat Hamadani. *Difa'iyat.* Trans. Qasim Ansari. Tehran: Intisharat-i Manuchihri, 1981–82.

———. *Tamhidat.* Ed. 'Afif 'Usayran. Tehran: Intisharat-i Manuchihri, 1991–92.

————. *Zubdat al-haqa'iq.* Ed. 'Afif 'Usayran. Tehran: Markaz-i Nashr-i Danishgahi, 2000–2001.

'Aziz ad-Din Nasafi. *Kashf al-haqa'iq.* Ed. Ahmad Mahdavi Damghani. Tehran: Shirkat-i Intisharat-i 'Ilmi va Farhangi, 2005.

Kitab al-insan al-kamil. Ed. Marijan Molé. Tehran: Intisharat-i Tahuri, 1983.

Baba Tahir. *Divan.* Ed. Manuchihr Adamiyat. Tehran: Intisharat-i Atiliya-yi Hunar-i Muhammad Salahshur, 2008–9.

Bahadur Shah Zafar. *Divan.* New Delhi: I'jaz Publishing House, 1997.

Bahram ibn Farhad, Farzana. *Sharistan-i chahar chaman.* Bombay: Matba'-yi Muzaffari, 1854.

Bahya Ben Joseph Ibn Paquda. *The Book of Direction to the Duties of the Heart.* Trans. Menahem Mansoor. London: Routledge & Kegan Paul, 1973.

Bausani, Alessandro. "Religion under the Mongols." In J. A. Boyle, ed., *The Cambridge History of Iran,* vol. 5. London and New York: Cambridge University Press, 1968.

Bar Hebraeus. *The Book of the Dove.* Trans. A. J. Wensinck. Leiden: E. J. Brill, 1919.

Beckwith, Christopher. *Warriors of the Cloisters: The Central Asian Origins of Science in the Medieval World.* Princeton, NJ: Princeton University Press, 2012.

The Bhagavad-Gita. Trans. Barbara Stoler Miller. New York: Bantam Books, 1986.

Bodhi, Bhikkhu, ed. *In the Buddha's Words: An Anthology of Discourses from the Pali Canon.* Somerville, MA:

Wisdom Publications, 2005.

————. *The Noble Eightfold Path: Way to the End of Suffering.* Onalaska, WA: Pariyatti Publishing, 2000.

Bonner, Anthony. *Doctor Illuminatus: A Ramon Llull Reader.* Princeton, NJ: Princeton University Press, 1993.

Bosch, F. D. K. *The Golden Germ: An Introduction to Indian Symbolism.* The Hague: Mouton, 1960.

Brock, Sebastian. *The Syriac Fathers on Prayer and the Spiritual Life.* Kalamazoo: Cistercian Publications Inc., 1987.

Bu 'Ali Shah Qalandar. *Divan.* Ed. Muhammad Siddiq Khan Shibli. Delhi: Kitabi Dunya, 2005.

Chodkiewicz, Michel. *Seal of the Saints: Prophethood and Sainthood in the Doctrine of Ibn 'Arabi.* Trans. Liadain Sherrard. Cambridge: The Islamic Texts Society, 1993.

Conze, Edward, trans. *Buddhist Wisdom.* New York: Vintage Books, 2001.

The Dhammapada. Trans. John Ross Carter and Mahinda Palihawadana. Oxford and New York: Oxford University Press, 2000.

Doniger, Wendy. *On Hinduism.* New York: Oxford University Press, 2014.

Duchesne-Guillemin, Jacques. *Symbols and Values in Zoroastrianism.* New York: Harper and Row, 1966.

Entry into the Realm of Reality. The Text: A Translation of the Gandavyuha, the final book of the Avatamsaka Sutra. Trans. Thomas Cleary. Boston and Shaftesbury: Shambhala Publications, 1989.

Ernst, Carl W. "India as a Sacred Islamic Land." In Donald S. Lopez, Jr., ed, *Religions of India in Practice.* Princeton, NJ: Princeton University Press, 1995.

————. "Traces of Shattari Sufism and Yoga in North Africa." Oriente Moderno XCII/2 (2013), 361–67.

Evagrius Ponticus. *Kephalaia Gnostika*. Trans. Ilaria Ramelli. Atlanta: SBL Press, 2015.

————. *The Praktikos and Chapters on Prayer*. Trans. John Eudes Bamberger OSCO. Trappist, KY: Cistercian Publications, 1972.

Fakhr ad-Din 'Iraqi, Shaykh. *Kulliyat*. Ed. Sa'id Nafisi. Tehran: Kitabkhana-yi Sana'i, n.d.

Farid ad-Din 'Attar, Shaykh. *Asrarnama*. Ed. Muhammahad Riza Shafi'i Kadkani. Tehran: Intisharat-i Sukhan, 2007–8.

————. *Divan*. Ed. Badi' az-Zaman Furuzanfar. Tehran: Mu'assasa-yi Intisharat-i Nigah, 1994–95.

————. *Ilahinama*. Ed. Muhammahad Riza Shafi'i Kadkani. Tehran: Intisharat-i Sukhan, 2008.

————. *Mantiq at-tayr*. Ed. Muhammahad Riza Shafi'i Kadkani. Tehran: Intisharat-i Sukhan, 2007.

————. *Musibatnama*. Ed. Muhammahad Riza Shafi'i Kadkani. Tehran: Intisharat-i Sukhan, 2007–8.

————. *Tazkirat al-awliya'*. Tehran: Intisharat-i Bihzad, 1994–95.

Mulla Firuz bin Kaus, ed. *The Desatir or Sacred Writings of the Ancient Persian Prophets; In the Original Tongue; Together with the Ancient Persian Version and Commentary of the Fifth Sasan*. 2 vols. Bombay: Courier Press, 1818.

Francis, Pope. *Laudato si': On Care for Our Common Home*. Huntington, IN: Our Sunday Visitor, 2015.

Ginzburg, Louis. *The Legends of the Jews*. Vol. 2. Philadelphia: The Jewish Publication Society of America, 1910.

Goitein, S. D. *Jews and Arabs: Their Contacts Through the Ages.* New York: Schocken Books, 1955.

Gregory of Nyssa, Saint. *Ascetical Works.* Trans. Virginia Woods Callahan. Washington DC: The Catholic University of America Press, 1966.

————. *From Glory to Glory.* Trans. Jean Daniélou. New York: Scribner, 1961.

Gregory the Great. *Moralia in Job.* N.p.: Ex Fontibus Company, 2012.

Habib 'Ali Shah, Khvaja. *Divan-i Habib.* Hyderabad: Khvaja Press, 2001.

Hamid Qalandar. *Khayr al-majalis.* Ed. Khaliq Ahmad Nizami. Aligarh: Muslim University, n.d.

Hasan Nizami, Khvaja. *Hindu mazhab ki ma'lumat.* Delhi: Halqa-yi Masha'ikh, 1927.

Hasan Sijzi, Amir. *Divan.* Hyderabad: Maktaba-yi Ibrahimiya, 1933.

————. *Fava'id al-fu'ad.* Lucknow: Naval Kishur, 1894.

Hatif Isfahani. *Divan.* Ed. Vahid Dastgirdi. Tehran: Intisharat-i Nigah, 2015.

Hierotheos (attributed). *The Book of the Holy Hierotheos.* Trans. F.S. Marsh. London: William and Norgate, 1927.

Hintze, Almut. *A Zoroastrian Liturgy: The Worship in Seven Chapters* (Yasna 35–41). Wiesbaden: Harrassowitz, 2007.

Husayn ibn Mansur al-Hallaj. *Diwan al-Hallaj wa yalihi akhbaruhu wa tawasinuhu.* Ed. Sa 'di Dannawi. Beirut: Dar Sadir, 2008.

Husayn Va'iz Kashifi, Mulla. *Anvar-i suhayli.* Allahabad: Lala Ram Narayan Lal, n.d.

———. *Futuvatnama-yi sultani*. Ed. Muhammad Jaʿfar Mahjub. Tehran: Intisharat-i Bunyad-i Farhang-i Iran, 1971.

———. *Rashahat*. Delhi: Naval Kishur, 1911.

The Hymns of Zoroaster. Trans. M. L. West. London and New York: I. B. Taurus, 2015.

Imdad Allah Muhajir Makki, Hajji. *Kulliyat-i Imdadiya*. Ed. Waqar ʿAli. Deoband: Maktaba-yi Thanvi, n.d.

———. *Ziyaʾ al-qulub*. Delhi: Matbaʿ-yi Mujtabaʾi, 1894.

Inayat Khan, Hazrat. *Complete Works, Original Texts: Lectures on Sufism 1923 II: July-December*. Ed. Munira van Voorst van Beest. London and The Hague: East-West Publications, 1988.

———. *Complete Works, Original Texts: Sayings I, Part I*. Ed. Munira van Voorst van Beest. London and The Hague: East-West Publications, 1989.

———. *Inayat git ratnavali*. Baroda: n.p., 1903.

———. *Minqar-i musiqar*. Allahabad: Indian Press, 1912.

———. *Social Gathekas* (unpublished papers).

———. *The Sufi Message of Hazrat Inayat Khan*. Vol. 5. London: Barrie and Rockliff, 1962.

———. "The Sufi Message" (pamphlet). London: n.p., n.d.

———. *Supplementary Papers* (unpublished papers).

Inayat Khan, Hazrat, and Westbrook, Jessie Duncan. *Diwan*. London: Sufi Publication Society, 1915.

Iqbalshah bin Sabiq Sijistani. *Chihil majlis*. Tehran: Intisharat-i Adib, 1987.

Isaac of Nineveh. *The Ascetical Homilies*. Trans. The Holy Transfiguration Monastery. Boston: The Holy Transfiguration Monastery, 2011.

———. *Mystic Treatises.* Trans. A. J. Wensinck. Amsterdam: Koninklijke Akademie van Wetenschappen, 1923.

Jalal ad-Din Rumi, Mawlana. *Fihi ma fih.* Ed. Badiʿ az-Zaman Furuzanfar. Tehran: Intisharat-i Danishgah-i Tihran, 1951.

———. *Kulliyat-i Shams.* Ed. Badiʿ az-Zaman Furuzanfar. 10 vols. Tehran: Intisharat-i Amir Kabir, 1999–2000.

———. *Masnavi-yi maʿnavi.* Tehran: Intisharat-i Bihnud, 1954.

———. *Taranaha-yi shurangiz-i Mawlavi.* Ed. Manuchihr ʿAlipur. Tehran: Intisharat-i Firdaws, 2002.

Jamal ad-Din Jamman, Shaykh. *Muntakhaba-yi divan-i Jamman.* Hyderabad: Matbaʿ-yi ʿAziz, n.d.

John Climacus. *The Ladder of Divine Ascent.* Trans. Colm Luibheid and Norman Russell. New York: Paulist Press, 1982.

Joseph ben Abraham Gikatilla, Rabbi. *Shaʾare orah: Gates of Light.* San Francisco: HarperCollins Publishers, 1994.

Kabir. *Kabir dohavali.* Ed. S. Nilotpal. New Delhi: Prabhat Paperbacks, 2016.

Kalim Allah Jahanabadi, Shah. *Kashkul-i Kalimi.* Delhi: Matbaʿ-i Mujtabaʾi, 1890–91.

———. *Muraqaʿa-yi Kalimi.* MS in the author's collection.

———. *Sawaʾ as-sabil.* Delhi: Astana Book Depot, n.d.

Kay Khusraw Isfandiyar, Mubad (att.). *Dabistan-i maza-hib.* Ed. Rahim Rizazada Malik. 2 vols. Tehran: Kitabkhana-yi Tahuri, 1983.

Khalidi, Tarif. *The Muslim Jesus: Sayings and Stories in Islamic Literature.* Cambridge MA: Harvard University Press, 2003.

Khuda-jui bin Namdar. *Jam-i Kay Khusraw*. Bombay: Matba'-yi Fazl ad-Din Kahamkar, 1868.

Khusraw Dihlavi, Amir. *Khamsa*. Ed. Amir Ahmad Ashrafi. Tehran: Intisharat-i Shaqa'iq, 1983–84.

Kugel, James L. *The Bible as It Was*. Cambridge, MA: The Belknap Press of Harvard University Press, 1997.

Kugle, Scott, and Ernst, Carl. *Sufi Meditation and Contemplation: Timeless Wisdom from Mughal India*. New Lebanon, NY: Suluk Press, 2012.

Lawson, Todd. *The Crucifixion and the Qur'an: A Study in the History of Muslim Thought*. Oxford: Oneworld Publications, 2009.

Lee, David. *Contextualization of Sufi Spirituality in Seventeenth- and Eighteenth-Century China: The Role of Liu Zhi (c. 1662–c. 1730)*. Eugene, OR: Pickwick Publications, 2015.

Liebeskind, Claudia. *Piety on Its Knees: Three Sufi Traditions in South Asia in Modern Times*. New Delhi: Oxford University Press, 1998.

Lobel, Diana. *A Sufi-Jewish Dialogue: Philosophy and Mysticism in Bahya Ibn Paquda's Duties of the Heart*. Philadelphia: University of Pennsylvania Press, 2007.

The Long Discourses of the Buddha. Trans. Maurice Walshe. Somerville, MA: Wisdom Publications, 2012.

López-Baralt, Luce. "Saint John of the Cross and Ibn 'Arabi: The Heart or Qalb as the Translucid and Ever-Changing Mirror of God." *Journal of the Muhyiddin Ibn 'Arabi Society*, vol. 28 (2000), 57–90.

The Mahabharata. Trans. Pratapa Chandra Ray. 9 volumes. Calcutta: Bharata Press, 1884–96.

Masson, J. L., and M. V. Patwardhan, *Aesthetic Rapture: The Rasadhyaya of the Natyasastra*. 2 vols. Poona: Deccan College, 1970.

Mahmud Shabistari, Shaykh. *Gulshan-i raz*. Ed. Ahmad Mujahid and Muhsin Kiyani. Tehran: Intisharat-yi Manuchihri and Silsila-yi Nashriyat-i Ma, 1992–93.

Mas'ud Bakk, Mawlana. *Divan*. Hyderabad: Matba'-yi Abu'l-'Ula'i, 1899–1900.

———. *Mir'at al-'arifin*. Hyderabad: Matba'-yi Mufid-i Dakan, 1892.

Mir Dard, Khvaja. *Divan*. Ed. Nasim Ahmad. New Delhi: Qaumi Kaunsil Bara'e Furogh-i Urdu Zaban, 2003.

Mir Taqi Mir. *Kulliyat*. Lahore: Sang-i Mil, 1995.

Mirza Mazhar Jan-i Janan, Shaykh. *Khutut*. Ed. and trans. Khaliq Anjum. Delhi: Maktaba-yi Burhan, 1962.

Moses Maimonides. *The Guide of the Perplexed*. Trans. Shlomo Pines. 2 vols. Chicago: The University of Chicago Press, 1963.

Muhammad Ahmad Sarmadi, Pir Sayyid. *Tazkira-yi Hazrat Sarmad Shahid*. Delhi: Kutubkhana-yi Sarmadi, n.d.

Muhammad al-Baqi, Khvaja (Khvaja Baqi Bi'llah). *'Irfani-yat-i Baqi*. Ed. Sayyid Nizam ad-Din Ahmad Kazimi Hayrat. Delhi: Khvaja Barqi Press, n.d.

Muhammad Chishti, Shaykh. *Majalis-i Hasaniya*. MS in the collection of Khvaja Rukn ad-Din Farrukh Chishti.

Muhammad Dara Shikuh, Shahzada. *Hasanat al-'arifin*. Trans. Muhammad 'Umar Khan. Lahore: Malik Fazl ad-Din et al. Tajiran-i Kutub-i Qaumi, n.d.

———. *Majma' al-bahrayn*. Ed. Sayyid Muhammad Riza Jalali Na'ini. Tehran: Nashr-i Nuqra, 1987–88.

————. *Risala-yi Haqq-numa*. Delhi: Matba'-yi Nami-yi Munshi Naval Kishur, n.d.

Muhammad Husayni Gisu Daraz, Sayyid. *Javahir al-'ushshaq*. Ed. Sayyid 'Ata Husayn. Hyderabad: Barqi Press, 1943.

————. *Majmu'a-yi yazda rasa'il*. Ed. Sayyid 'Ata Husayn. Hyderabad: Intizami Press, n.d.

————. (attributed). *Mi'raj al-'ashiqin*. Ed. Maulana 'Abd al-Haqq. Aurangabad: Taj Press, 1924–25.

————. *Sharh-i risala-yi Qushayriya*. Ed. Sayyid 'Ata Husayn. Hyderabad: Barqi Press, 1942.

————. *Wujud al-'ashiqin*. Moradabad, U.P.: Matba'-yi Gulzar-i Ibrahim, n.d.

Muhammad Gul Ahmadpuri. *Takmila-yi siyar al-awliya'*. MS in collection of the late Khaliq Ahmad Nizami.

Muhammad Makhdum Husayn, Mawlana. *Mizan at-tawhid*. Ed. Sayyid Muhammad Abu Hashim al-Madani. Hyderabad: Matba'-yi Burhaniya, 1893–94.

Muhammad Munir ad-Din Mahmudi. *Shajarat al-Mahmud*. Hyderabad: Matba'-yi Gulzar, 1886–87.

Muhammad ibn Ishaq. *The Life of Muhammad: A Translation of Ibn Ishaq's Sirat Rasul Allah*. Trans. Alfred Guillaume. Oxford: Oxford University Press, 1955.

Muhammad ibn Mubarak Kirmani, Sayyid (Amir Khwurd). *Siyar al-awliya'*. Delhi: Matba'-yi Muhibb-i Hind, 1884–85.

Muhammad ibn Munavvar. *Asrar at-tawhid fi maqamat ash-Shaykh Abi Sa'id*. Ed. Muhammad Riza Shafi'i Kadkani. Tehran: Intisharat-i Agah, 1987. 2 vols.

Muhammad ibn Sirin. *Tafsir al-ahlam*. Beirut: Dar Sadir, 2010.

Muhammad Nasir 'Andalib, Khvaja. *Nala-yi 'Andalib*. 2 vols. Bhopal: Matba'-yi Shahjahani, 1893.

Muhammahad Riza Shafi'i Kadkani. *Daftar-i rawshanayi: az miras-'irfani-yi Bayazid Bistami*. Tehran: Intisharat-i Sukhan, 2005–6.

———. *Nivishta bar darya: az miras-i 'irfani-yi Abu'l-Hasan Kharaqani*. Tehran: Intisharat-i Sukhan, 2005–6.

———. *Sha'ir-i ayina-ha: barrasi-yi sabk-i Hindi va shi'r-i Bidil*. Tehran: Mu'assasa-yi Instisharat-i Agah, 1987–88.

Muhammad Tahir Ghani. *Divan*. Kanpur: Naval Kishur, 1876.

Muhammad Taqi Niyazi, Shah ('Aziz Miyan). *Raz-i muhabbat*. Bareilly: Muhammad Ja'far Nizami Niyazi, n.d.

———. *Raz-i niyaz*. Bareilly: Hamid Hasan Qadiri, 1944.

———. *Raz-i takhliq*. No publication data.

Muhammad Ziya' al-Hasan Jili Kalimi, Sayyid. *Kalam-i Ziya'*. Hyderabad: Maktaba Rahmaniya, 2003.

Muhsin Fayz Kashani, Mulla. *Divan-i kamil*. Ed. Sayyid 'Ali Shafi'i. Tehran: Nashr-i Chakama, 1994–95.

Muhyi ad-Din Ibn 'Arabi, Shaykh. *Fusus al-hikam*. Beirut: Dar al-Kitab al-'Arabi, 1980.

———. *al-Futuhat al-makkiya*. 4 vols. Beirut: Dar Sadir, 1968.

———. *Mawaqi' an-nujum wa matali' ahillat al-asrar wa al-'ulum*. Ed. Muhammad Badr ad-Din an-Na'dani. Cairo: Matba'at as-Sa'ada, 1907.

———. *The Secrets of Voyaging (Kitab al-isfar 'an nata'ij al-asfar)*. Trans. Angela Jaffray. Oxford: Anqa Publishing, 2015.

———. *Tanbihat 'ala 'uluw al-haqiqat al-Muhammadiya wa yalihi Ruh al-quds fi muhasabat an-nafs*. Ed. 'Asim

Ibrahim al-Kayyali. Beirut: Dar al-Kutub al-'Ilmiya, 2007.

———. *Tarjuman al-ashwaq.* Beirut: Dar Sadir, 1966.

———. *Tarjuman al-ashwaq.* Trans. R. A. Nicholson. London: Theosophical Publishing House, 1978.

Mu'in ad-Din Chishti, Khvaja (attributed). *Divan-i Gharib Navaz.* Delhi: Kutubkhana-yi Naziriya, 1958.

———. (attributed). *Mutarjam maktub Khvaja Mu'in ad-Din Chishti 'alayhi rahma.* Moradabad: Matba'-yi Ihtishamiya, 1899.

Murata, Sachiko. *Chinese Gleams of Sufi Light: Wang Tai-yü's Great Learning of the Pure and Real and Liu Chih's Displaying the Concealment of the Real Realm.* Albany: State University of New York Press, 2000.

Muslih ibn 'Abd Allah Sa'di. *Kulliyat.* Ed. Baha' ad-Din Khurramshahi. Tehran: Intisharat-i Dustan, 2010.

The Nag Hammadi Scriptures. Ed. Marvin Meyer. New York: HarperCollins, 2007.

Najm ad-Din Kubra, Shaykh. *Die Fawa'ih al-Gamal wa Fawatih al-Galal (Kitab fawa'ih al-jamal wa fawatih al-jalal).* Ed. Fritz Meier. Wiesbaden: Franz Steiner Verlag, 1957.

Netton, Ian Richard. *Allah Transcendent: Studies in the Structure and Semiotics of Islamic Philosophy, Theology, and Cosmology.* London and New York: Routledge, 1989.

The New English Bible, with The Apocrypha. New York: Oxford University Press, 1971.

Nicholson, Reynold Alleyne. *Studies in Islamic Mysticism.* Cambridge: The University Press, 1921.

Nizam al-Din Awrangabadi, Shah. *Nizam al-qulub.* Delhi: Matba'-yi Mujtaba'i, 1891–92.

Nizami, Khaliq Ahmad. *The Life and Times of Shaikh Nizamuddin Aulia*. Delhi: Idarah-i Adabiyat, 1991.

Nur ad-Din 'Abd ar-Rahman Jami, Shaykh. *Lava'ih*. Ed. Yann Richard. Tehran: Intisharat-i Asatir, 2004–5.

———. *Nafahat al-'uns*. Ed. Mahmud 'Abidi. Tehran: Intisharat-i Ittila'at, 1991–92.

Nur ad-Din Jahangir, Padishah. *The Tuzuk-i Jahangiri or Memoirs of Jahangir*. Trans. A. Rogers and H. Beveridge. London: The Royal Asiatic Society, 1909.

Nur al-Hasan Sahasvani, Sayyid, ed. *Naghmat-i sama'*. Badaun: Matbu'at-i Nizami, 1934.

'Obadyah Maimonides. *The Treatise of the Pool: Al-Maqala al-Hawdiyya*. Trans. Paul Fenton. London: The Octagon Press, 1981.

Origen. *On First Principles*. Trans. Henri De Lubac. New York: Harper and Row, 1966.

Palacios, Miguel Asin. *Islam and the Divine Comedy*. Trans. Harold Sutherland. London: Frank Cass & Co., 1968.

Patanjali, attributed. *Yoga: Discipline of Freedom (The Yoga Sutra)*. Trans. Barbara Stoler Miller. Berkeley: University of California Press, 1995.

Perek Shirah. Trans. Rabbi Natan Slifkin. New York: Zoo Torah, 2009.

Philotheus. *The History of the Blessed Virgin Mary and The History of the Likeness of Christ*. Trans. E. A. Wallis Budge. London: Luzac and Co., 1899.

Pistis Sophia. Trans. G.R.S. Mead. New York: Garber Communications, 1984.

The Prophets: Nevi'im, A new translation of the Holy Scriptures according to the Masoretic text, Second Section. Philadelphia: The Jewish Publication Society of America, 1978.

Pseudo-Dionysius. *The Complete Works*. Trans. Colm
Luibheid. New York: Paulist Press, 1987.

Qutb ad-Din Bakhtiyar Kaki (att.). *Divan*. Kanpur: Munshi
Naval Kishur, 1915.

Rahula, Walpola. *What the Buddha Taught*. New York:
Grove Press, 1974.

Rangaswami, Sudhakshina. *The Roots of Vedanta: Selections from Sankara's Writings*. New Delhi: Penguin
Books, 2012.

Rashid ad-Din Mawdud Lala, Shaykh. *Mukhbir al-awliya'*. MS in the collection of Khvaja Rukn ad-Din
Farrukh Chishti.

Rawson, Joseph Nadin. *The Katha Upanishad*. London:
Oxford University Press, 1934.

Rig Veda. Trans. Wendy Doniger. London: Penguin
Books, 1981.

Risala-yi chahar o chaharda khanvada. MS in the author's
collection.

Ruzbihan Baqli Shirazi, Shaykh. *Sharh-i shathiyat*. Ed.
Henry Corbin. Tehran: Kitabkhana-yi Tahuri, 1981.

Sacred Books of the East: Pahlavi Texts, Part I. Trans. E.
W. West. New Delhi: Motilal Banarsidass, 1977.

Sacred Books of the East: Pahlavi Texts, Part V. Trans. E.
W. West. New Delhi: Motilal Banarsidass, 1987.

Sacred Books of the East: The Zend-Avesta, Parts I and II.
Trans. James Darmesteter. New York: Christian Literature Company, 1898.

Sacred Books of the East: The Zend-Avesta, Part II. Trans.
James Darmesteter. New Delhi: Motilal Banarsidas,
1981.

Sacred Books of the East: The Zend-Avesta, Part III. Trans.

L. H. Mills. New Delhi: Motilal Banarsidas, 1981.

Sadiq Hidayat. *Taranaha-yi Khayyam.* Los Angeles: Intisharat-i Shirkat-i Kitab, 2014.

Salahi, 'Imran. *Ru'yaha-yi mard-i nilufari: ahwal va afkar va asar-i Sa'id Sarmad Kashani.* Tehran: Intisharat-i Nahid, 1991.

Scheindlin, Raymond P. *The Gazelle: Medieval Hebrew Poems on God, Israel, and the Soul.* Philadelphia: The Jewish Publication Society, 1991.

Senzaki, Nyogen. *Sufism and Zen.* Tucson: Ikhwan Press, 1972.

Shahab ad-Din Ahmad ibn Mansur Sam'ani, *Rawh al-arvah fi sharh asma' al-Malik al-Fattah.* Ed. Najib Mayil Haravi. Tehran: Shirkat-i Instisharat-i 'Ilmi va Farhangi, 1989.

Shahab ad-Din Yahya Suhravardi. *Majmu'a-yi musannafat-i Shaykh-i Ishraq.* Ed. Henry Corbin and Seyyed Hossein Nasr. 3 vols. Tehran: Pizhuhishgah-i 'Ulum-i Insani va Farhangi, 1993.

Shams ad-Din Ahmad Aflaki. *Manaqib al-'arifin.* Ed. Tahsin Yaziji. 2 vols. Tehran: Dunya Kitab, 1963–64.

Shams ad-Din Muhammad Hafiz, Khvaja. *Divan.* Ed. Muhammad Qazvini and Qasim Ghani. Tehran: Nashr-i Arvin, 1994.

Shantideva. *The Way of the Bodhisattva.* Trans. Padmakara Translation Group. Boston and London: Shambhala, 2006.

Sharaf ad-Din Ahmad Yahya Manayri, Makhdum. *Maktubat-i sadi.* Patna: Khuda Bakhsh Oriental Public Library, 1994.

Siraj ad-Din Siraj Awrangabadi. *Kulliyat.* Ed. 'Abd al-Qadir Sarvari. Hyderabad: Majlis-i Isha'at-i Dakkani Makhtutat, 1939.

Stolk, Sirkar van, and Dunlop, Daphne. *Memories of a Sufi Sage: Hazrat Inayat Khan.* The Hague: East-West Publication Fonds B.V., 1967.

Upanishads. Trans. Patrick Olivelle. Oxford University Press, 1996.

———. *The Upanishads.* Trans. Juan Mascaro. New York: Penguin, 1965.

———. *Sixty Upanishads of the Veda.* Trans. Paul Deussen, V. M. Bedekar, and G. B. Palsule. New Delhi: Motilal Banarsidas, 1997.

———. *Eight Upanishads with the Commentary of Shankaracharya.* Trans. Swami Gambhirananda. Mayavati (India): Advaita Ashrama, 2014.

———. *Sirr-i Akbar.* Trans. Muhammad Dara Shikuh. Ed. Tara Chand and Muhammad Riza Jalali Na'ini. 2 volumes. Tehran: Intisharat-i 'Ilmi, 1989–90.

'Umar bin Muhammad Suhravardi. *'Awarif al-ma'arif.* Ed. Ahmad 'Abd ar-Rahim as-Sayih and Tawfiq 'Ali Wahba. 2 vols. Cairo: Maktaba ath-Thaqafa ad-Diniya, 2006.

'Umar Khayyam. *Les Quatrains de Khèyam.* Trans. J. B. Nicolas. Paris: Imprimerie impériale, 1867.

Van Bladel, Kevin. "The Bactrian Background of the Barmakids." In Akasoy, Anna, Burnett, Charles, and Yoeli Tlalim, Ronir, ed. *Islam and Tibet: Interactions along the Musk Routes.* Farnham, England, and Burlington, VT: Ashgate, 2011.

Vasistha (attributed). *The Supreme Yoga: A New Translation of the Yoga Vasistha.* Trans. Swami Venkatesananda. 2 vols. New Delhi: New Age Books, 2013.

Vaziri, Mostafa. *Buddhism in Iran: An Anthropological Approach to Traces and Influences.* New York: Palgrave Macmillan, 2012.

Ward, Benedicta, trans. *The Desert Fathers: Sayings of the Early Christian Monks*. London: Penguin Books, 2003.

Wensinck, A.J.. *Bar Hebraeus's Book of the Dove Together with Some Chapters from His Ethikon*. Leiden: E.J. Brill, 1919.

The Wisdom Books: Job, Proverbs, and Ecclesiastes. Trans. Robert Alter. New York. W. W. Norton & Company, 2010.

Writings from the Philokalia on the Prayer of the Heart. Trans. E. Kadbloubovsky and G. E. H. Palmer. London: Faber and Faber, 1992.

The Yoga of Delight, Wonder, and Astonishment: A Translation of the Vijnana-bhairava. Trans. Jaideva Singh. Albany: State University of New York Press, 1991.

Yoga Vasishtha. Trans. Swami Venkatesananda. New Delhi: New Age Books, 2013.

———. *Jug bashast*. Trans. Muhammad Dara Shikuh. Ed. Tara Chand and Sayyid Amir Hasan 'Abidi. Aligarh: Danishgah-i Islami-yi Aligar, 1968.

Zand-Akasih: Iranian or Greater Bundahisn. Trans. Behramgore Tehmuras Anklesaria. Bombay: Rahnuma Mazdayasnan Sabha, 1956.

Zaehner, R.C.. *Hindu and Muslim Mysticism*. London: The Athlone Press, 1960.

Zartusht Bahram bin Pazhdu. *Zaratushtnama*. Ed. and trans. Friderikh Aleksandrovich Rosenberg. St. Petersburg: Académie Impériale des Sciences 1904.

Ziya' ad-Din Nakhshabi. *Silk as-suluk*. Tehran: Kitabfurushi-yi Zavvar, 1991.

The Zohar: Pritzker Edition. Trans. Daniel C. Matt, Nathan Wolski, and Joel Hecker. 12 volumes (to date). Stanford: Stanford University Press, 2008-2017.

Index

A

Aaron 129, 139, 156
Abba Isaac *See* Isaac of Ni-
    nevah.
'Abbas ibn Yusuf Shakli 254
Abbasid Empire 46
'Abd al-Karim al-Qushayri
    31, 65, 67–68, 141, 148,
    160–161, 165, 224, 267,
    274–275, 290, 292,
    295–296, 308, 317, 328
'Abd al-Karim Jili 169
'Abd Allah Ansari 85–86, 319
'Abd Allah Faraj 69
'Abd al-Qadir Bidil 20, 71–72,
    75, 84, 191, 266, 276,
    278, 302, 317, 329.
'Abd al-Qadir Jilani (Sublime
    Defender) 103, 149,
    226, 243, 249, 312
'Abd al-Quddus Gangohi 4
'Abd ar-Rahman as-Sulami
    69, 275, 317
'Abd ar-Rahman Chishti 4,
    199, 304, 317
'Abd ar-Razzaq Kashani 116,
    284, 317
Abhay Chand 132
ablution 131, 230–231. *See
    also* purification, water
Abode of Song 101
Abraham (Friend of God) x,
    14, 85, 129–130, 156,
    217, 229, 235, 247–248

Abraham Abu'l-'Afiya
    131–132
Abraham ha-Hasid 131
Abraham of Nathpar 197, 303
absence 65–66, 94, 218, 242,
    248, 255
absorption, mystical 58, 197;
    absorption in absorp-
    tion 117; absorption
    in God's unity 226;
    absorptions with form
    71; four formless ab-
    sorptions 72
Abu 'Abd Allah Harith Muha-
    sibi 130
Abu 'Abd Allah Ramli 141
Abu 'Ali Daqqaq 68, 161
Abu Bakr (the Sincere) 37,
    237, 277, 308, 310, 317
Abu Bakr al-Kalabadhi 76,
    277, 317
Abu Bakr Kattani 64
Abu Bakr Wasiti 168
Abu Hashim Madani 78
Abu'l-'Abbas Dinawari 16
Abu'l-Darda 70
Abu'l-Fazl 'Allami 91, 280, 318
Abu'l-Futuh 38, 72, 84
Abu'l-Hasan Kharaqani
    67–68, 71, 90, 226, 329
Abu'l-Majd Majdud Sana'i 16,
    68, 76–77, 79, 85, 89,
    129, 140, 176, 224, 230,
    254, 265, 275, 277–279,
    286, 290, 299, 308–309,
    313, 318
Abu'l-Qasim Firdawsi 116,
    284, 318
Abu'l-Qasim Sabzavari 133

337

Index

Brahma 7; Brahmanist monotheism 7. *See also*
Hinduism
Brahmin 37, 65, 92. *See also*
Hinduism
breath 14, 67, 69, 113, 121,
124, 176, 181, 183–184,
192, 201, 225; breath of
all breaths 40; breath
of life 31; Breath of
Mercy 183; flame of
breath 117; Gabriel's
breath 182; practices
of breath control 132;
the One's own Breath
184. *See also* air, wind
Brhadaranyaka Upanishad
33, 268
brilliance 142, 154, 216. *See
also* light
Bu 'Ali Shah Qalandar 191,
282, 302, 321
Buddha (Tathagata) 45, 49,
55, 59, 63, 77, 79, 217,
319–320, 326, 332;
Budhasaf 45, 270: He
Who Has Thus Gone
59, 63, 65–68, 75, 83,
85–86; Shakyamuni 45,
48; Siddartha 55–59.
See also Buddhism
buddhi 27, 38. *See also* intellect
Buddhism 45, 46, 49–50,
92, 321, 334: Bud-
dhist temples 46;
Sufi-Buddhist contacts
50. *See also bakhshi*,
Bodhisattva, Bud-
dha, Buddhists, Dalai

Lama, *Diamond Sutra,*
Middle Way, monk,
mindfulness, Noble
Path, Zen, individual
Buddhists by name
Buddhists 51, 92. *See also*
bakhshi, Buddhism,
individual Buddnists
by name
Bu'l-Fazl Hasan 38
Bundahishn 99, 280. *See also*
Zoroastrianism
Burkh 143
burning bush 138
Buzurgmihr 89

C

cat 191, 302
certainty 66, 224–225, 308–309
chain of transmission 90;
shining chain 200. *See
also* emanation
Chandogya Upanishad 33, 268
chant(ing) 170, 172, 198, 210;
chants of the seraphim
201. *See also* hymn,
mantra, *Nist hasti
magar Yazdan,* Psalms,
recitation, song, *zikr*
chevalier 67, 123. *See also*
chivalry
child 55, 137, 165, 175–176,
207, 211, 224; children
160, 197, 211; children
of Adam 153. *See also
under Jesus*, Christ
child
China 45, 49, 326, 330
chin mudra 8

Index

Index

Index

Index

dervish 67, 102, 133, 143;
dervishhood 8. *See
also* qalandar, Sufi
desert father 181, 201, 335.
See also ascetic, Christians, ecstatics, hermit,
seclusion, solitude
desire xi, 11, 26, 15, 20, 33,
38, 66, 70, 143, 171,
188, 217, 224, 232, 242,
272; confused desires
40; desire's maze 26;
desire to be known 26;
eyes of desire ix; fire of
desire 113; movement
of desire 26; shapes of
desire 58; veil of desire
232. *See also* heart,
hunger, longing, love
Destructive Spirit 99. *See also*
demon, devil, Satan
detachment 69, 116
devas 7. *See also* angels
devil 57, 107–108. *See also*
demon, Destructive
Spirit, imp, Satan
devotion 3, 5, 26, 242; devotee 132, 254; devout
mendicants 219. *See
also* faith, love, piety,
service
devotions 64. *See also* prayer
dharma 60, 77; non-dharma
77; wheel of the dharma 63
Diamond Sutra 75–79
Dionysius the Areopagite
200, 332
discernment 39, 58, 261; dis-

cerning heart 255
discipline 47–49, 114, 331
dispossession 94, 116–117;
the dispossessed 242
Divine Comedy 167, 331
djinn 57, 147
doctrine 37, 49, 90, 321:
doctrine of the Trinity
168; Oriental doctrine
of light and darkness
90. *See also* belief,
creed, religion
dream 32, 38, 51, 79, 123,
209, 247
drunkenness 19, 75, 133, 148,
190, 192; drunkard x.
See also wine
duality 26. *See also* opposites,
multiplicity

E

eagle 210
earth 13, 20–21, 27, 33, 41, 57,
69–70, 79, 85–86, 91,
93, 99, 101, 107–108,
116, 121–125, 129, 132,
155, 157, 162, 181–183,
188, 198, 200–201, 203,
208, 215–216, 219, 223,
229, 231–232, 248, 256;
earthly humility 66; new
earth 200; virgin earth
176. *See also* clay
East, the 49, 131, 207, 209,
211–212, 332; East
Wind 161; Eastern
music 147. *See also*
Orient, individual
place names in the East

Index

Eckhart, Meister 50
ecstasy 131, 150, 172, 202;
   ecstatic confessions
   203; ecstatic Kabbal-
   ah 131–132; ecstatic
   speech 197. *See also*
   bliss, ecstatics, exaltation, glory, joy, rapture,
   samadhi
ecstatics 129. *See also* dervish,
   ecstasy, mystics, qalandar
ecumenism 133
Eden 3, 142. *See also* Garden
   of Paradise, paradise.
ego 57, 67, 70, 76–77, 102,
   140, 159, 209, 254;
   endarkened ego 188;
   illusory self 76. *See
   also nafs*, self, selfishness, selflessness,
   self-regard
Egypt(ian) 89, 130–131, 137–
   140, 166, 183, 207–210;
   Egyptian Hasidim 131;
   Egyptian Jews 131. *See
   also* Exodus, individual
   Egyptians by name
elements x, 27, 69–70, 93,
   124; elemental castles
   45; elementals 122. *See
   also* air, earth, ether,
   fire, water
elephant 3, 198
Elisabeth, Saint 176
emanation 90, 99, 211, 216.
   See also chain of transmission, light
emptiness 81, 83–85, 217,
   242. *See also* nirvana,

space, void
enemy 67, 109, 123, 209, 255.
   See also enmity
enlightenment 67, 70. *See also*
   awakened one, illumi-
   nation, light, realization, revelation
enmity 66. *See also* enemy
Enoch 92, 156
Ephrem the Syrian 175–176
esotericism 131, 169; esoteric
   reality xi. *See also* gnosis,
   mysticism
essence 8, 16, 19, 21, 31–34,
   76, 84, 91, 142, 169,
   176, 183, 216–217, 232,
   247; divine essence 16;
   essence of humanity
   21; essence of the es-
   sence 31, 34; quintes-
   sence 71
Eternal, the 71, 139, 175, 231,
   256. *See also* eternity
eternity 32, 56, 72, 77, 115,
   125, 175, 202; eternal
   way 156; everlasting-
   ness 27, 64; Mirror
   of Eternity 21; ocean
   of the eternity 32;
   pre-eternity 231. *See
   also* Eternal
ether 27
Evagrius Ponticus 187–189,
   199, 298, 300–301, 304,
   322
Eve 26, 142, 154, 286, 293–294
evil 27, 58, 65–66, 99, 101,
   108, 123, 137, 160,
   182, 187–191, 200;

Index

glory 14, 40, 83, 115, 141, 177, 203, 323; glories of the Face 142, 182; Light of Glory 115–116. *See also* ecstasy, glorification, Sakina

gnosis x, 26, 137, 191; secrets of gnosis 144. *See also* esotericism, gnostic, knowledge, mysticism, wisdom

gnostics ix–x, 64, 78, 154, 197–203, 210, 243, 248, 254, 256. *See also* arhat, 'arif, gnosis, Hasidim, hesychasts, mystics, sages, wise ones

golden age 123; Spain's Golden Age 130

Golden Embryo *See* Hiranyagarbha

good, the xii, 27, 37–38, 48, 58, 63, 65–67, 99, 102, 105, 107, 109, 113–114, 160, 181–182, 193, 200, 237; good deeds 101; good thoughts 101; good will 65; good words 67, 101, 181–182, 184. *See also* compassion, foregiveness, love, mercy

Good Mind, the 100–101, 108. *See also* Vohuman

Gorakhnath 4

Gospels 167, 168, 253; Gospel of John 182, 215; Gospel of Thomas 200, 210–211, 304, 306. *See also* Bible, Christianity, Jesus Christ, New Testament, Luke, Matthew

grapes xi; people of the grape xii. *See also* wine

Greatest Shaykh *See* Muhyi ad-Din Ibn 'Arabi

Great Soul 19–21, 39; Great Soul's body 20. *See also* Hiranyagarbha, soul, Universal Soul

Great Words 182. *See also* angels, intelligences

Greece xi, 92; Hellenistic West 46. *See also* individual Greeks by name

green 95, 122, 256; green light 94; Green One 144. *See also* Khizr

Gregory Bar Hebraeus 167, 197, 199, 203, 303

Gregory of Nyssa 175, 201, 323

Gregory of Sinai 200

Gregory the Great 198, 323

guardians 91; guardianship of water 122

guidance ix, xiv, 51, 56, 68, 75, 137, 156, 159, 211; guidance on the straight path 232; guiding light 188. *See also* guides, Khizr, Spirit of Guidance

guide x, 8, 116, 156, 208, 254, 271; Guide of the Way 250; guide to the truth 69. *See also* guidance, Khizr.

Index

Index

Index

Ramadan 235–236, 241. *See also* fasting

Ramayana 5

Rambam 139, 142

rapture 32, 70–71, 150, 327. *See also* bliss, ecstasy, exaltation, samadhi

rasa 31–32. *See also* essence

Rashid ad-Din Mawdud Lala 305, 332

Rashid ad-Din Maybudi 308

reality xi–xii, 7, 41, 100, 113, 116, 162, 177, 220, 225, 237, 248, 254; Muhammadan reality 19. *See also* truth

realization 6, 34, 50, 59, 66, 100. *See also* enlightenment, wakefulness

recitation xi–xii, 7, 41, 50, 86, 93, 117, 131, 141, 148, 153, 168, 170, 197–198, 201, 230, 253, 262; heart's recitation 198. *See also* chant, mantra, *Nist hasti magar Yazdan, zikr*

recollection 199; recollection of the Beloved 133. *See also* remembrance

red 95, 134. *See also* colors, crimson

reed 137, 150

reflection 40, 94, 249, 271. *See also* mirror

religion ix, xi–xiii, 4–6, 34, 49, 90, 121, 129–130, 133, 140, 149, 167, 199, 217, 235, 253–255; feuds over religion 254; goal of all religions xi; religion of love xii, 149; religious pluralism 5, 46; *See also* belief, creed, devotion, doctrine, faith, monotheism, individual religions by name

remembrance, divine 8, 26, 93, 113–114, 154, 162, 209–210, 219, 221, 224–226; remembrance of the departed 70. *See also* chant, contemplation, *La ilaha illa'Llah,* meditation, recollection, *zikr*

renunciation 45–46, 49, 65, 165, 242. *See also* asceticism, repentance, sacrifice

repentance 3, 64, 140, 142, 162, 185, 187, 193, 193, 197, 241. *See also* penance, renunciation, salvation

resurrection 49, 168. *See also* ascension, Day of Resurrection, Jesus Christ

revelation xi–xii, 3, 6, 15, 19–20, 32, 38, 84, 94, 99–101, 124, 130, 138–139, 143, 150, 155, 161, 166, 169, 175, 192, 207, 217–219, 236, 253–255; revelation of Peter 177; revelation of the Qur'an 217; the

Index

220, 224, 253; spiritual discipline 47, 114; spiritual embryo 210; spiritual forgetting 208; spiritual perception xiii, 94. *See also* mysticism, spirit
stars 21, 79, 107–108, 115, 155, 226; constellation 93; heaven of fixed stars 95; starry book 116; starry chain of being 200
stations xiv, 26, 39, 66, 100, 116–117, 141, 166, 197, 229. *See also maqams*
Subhuti 75
Sublime Defender *See* 'Abd al-Qadir Jilani
Succor of the Poor *See* Mu'in ad-Din Chishti.
Sudhana 78
suffering 55–56, 65, 85, 102, 138, 162, 168, 209, 230, 321. *See also* crucifixion
Sufis ii, ix, xi, xiii, 6, 8, 45, 64, 76, 78, 90, 92–93, 95, 114, 129–133, 141–142, 165–168, 198, 215, 218–219, 224, 237; early Sufis 130, 166; Muslim Sufis 8, 167; Sufi martyr 167; Sufis of Islam 139, 141, 166;. *See also* dervish, mystics, qalandar, Sufism, individual Sufis by name
Sufism 3–8, 45, 49–51, 57, 69,

77, 79, 94, 129–132, 165–166, 215, 232, 322, 324, 326, 330, 333–334; Indian Sufism 4; Jewish Sufi movement 130–131, 287; lineages of Sufism 220; Muridiya Order 8; Sufi commentary on the Bhagavad Gita 4; Sufi-Buddhist 50; Sufi Hasidism 131; Sufi-Buddhist contacts 50; Sufi philosophy of Illumination 92; Sufi's religion xii; Sufi School of Love 167; Sufi symbols 167; Zoroastrian Sufism 95. *See also* Chishtis, *La ilaha illa'Llah*, mysticism, Naqshbandi Order, patched robe, Qadiri Order, Saqi, Sanusis, Shattari Order; Sufis, *zikr*
Sufyan Sawri 78, 247
Suhravardi *See* Shahab ad-Din Yahya Suhravardi.
Sultan Ibrahim *See* Ibrahim bin Adham
suluk 8, 47. *See also* Sufism
sun 14, 19, 33, 40, 55, 59, 85, 91, 93, 142, 154–155, 201, 216, 226; angel of the sun 91; Sun of Truth 216; sunny affection 66. *See also* light